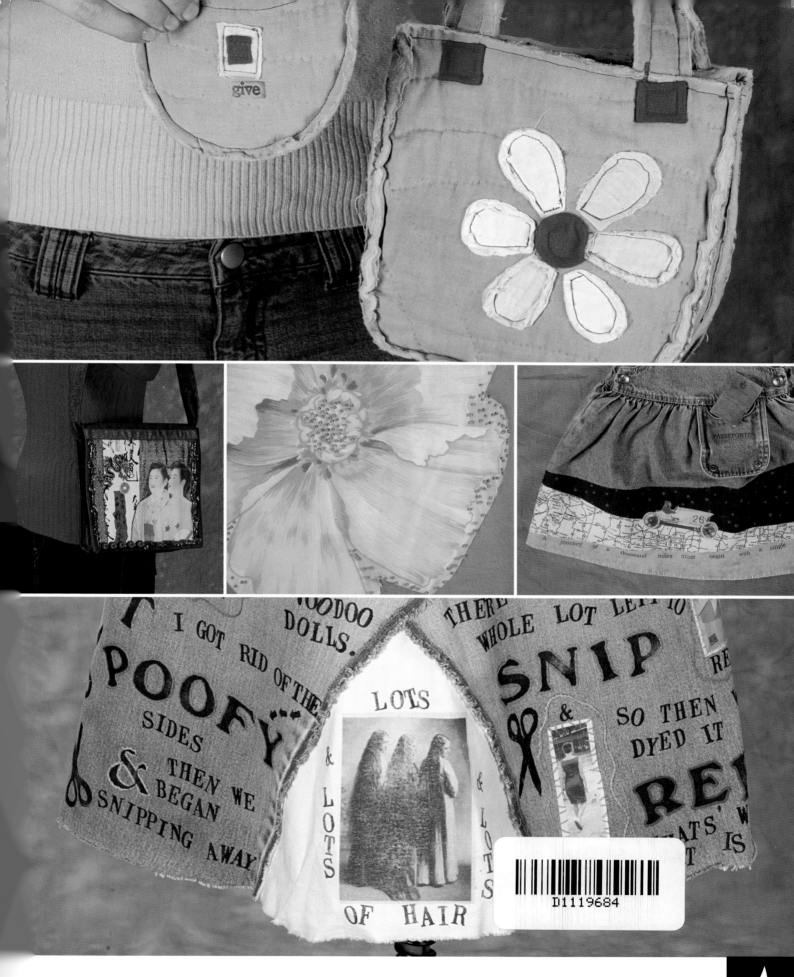

give

I GOT RID OF THE ... VOODOO DOLLS. THERE ... WHOLE LOT LEFT TO

SPOOFY ... SIDES & THEN WE BEGAN SNIPPING AWAY

LOTS & LOTS OF HAIR

SNIP & SO THEN ... DYED IT RE ... THATS' ... IS

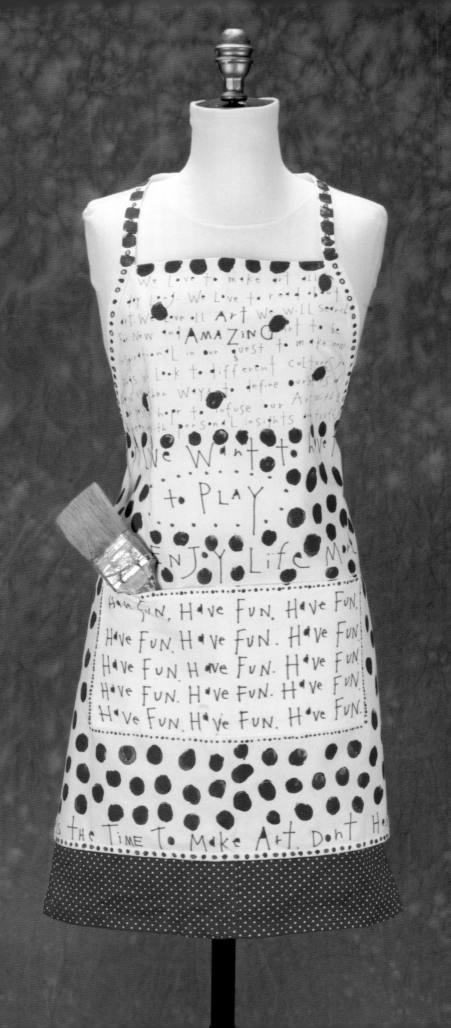

NEW TECHNIQUES FOR

wearable art

QUARRY BOOKS

creative ideas for transforming clothes and accessories

Ricë Freeman-Zachery

First published in the United States of America by
Quarry Books, an imprint of
Rockport Publishers, Inc.
33 Commercial Street
Gloucester, Massachusetts 01930-5089
Telephone: 978.282.9590
Fax: 978.282.2742
www.rockpub.com

Library of Congress Cataloging-in-Publication Data
Freeman-Zachery, Ricë.
   New techniques for wearable art : creative ideas for transforming clothes and
accessories / Ricë Freeman-Zachery.
      p.   cm.
   ISBN 1-59253-075-3 (pbk.)
   1. Clothing and dress—Alteration. 2. Textile crafts. 3. Wearable art. I. Title.
TT550.F74 2004
646.4—dc22   2004002793

ISBN 1-59253-075-3

10 9 8 7 6 5 4 3 2

Design: Yee Design
Photography: Andrew Swaine Photography
Template: Lorraine Dey Studio

Printed in Singapore

To Earl, who makes it all possible.

contents

Elaborate Projects

foreword

It takes courage to wear your art on your sleeve, but you can do it with style given the guidance offered in this book by Ricë Freeman-Zachery. Trust Ricë to guide us all into more art-filled living through the medium of wearable art! She lives inside her creations—literally—and inspires us to do the same by opening up our minds to more creative possibilities than we might have imagined on our own.

A journal that functions as a skirt? Why not? Using alphabet stamps and a few favorite embellishments, you can transform items from your wardrobe into artistic wearable expressions. Put it out there! Share your political views on a pair of jeans; dress up a funky old pair of sneakers with paint and beads; use collage techniques on a T-shirt— again, why not? It's a bold concept, but one that's needed in our increasingly cold, technology-driven society.

I admire Ricë for sharing her unique vision for wearable art with the rest of us. Her designs and techniques are timely and fashionable, yet nostalgic as well, reaching a part of our souls that longs to be touched by human hands. Using the methods she describes, you can do the same. Turn plain clothes into creative artwear—and make an indelible impression on yourself and those around you.

–Sharilyn Miller

Sharilyn Miller is the editor-in-chief of Belle Armoire, *a quarterly magazine covering new work and trends in wearable art. She is the author of* Rubber Stamped Jewelry *(North Light Books, 2003),* The Stamp Artist's Project Book *(Rockport Publishers, 2001) and* Stamp Art *(Rockport Publishers, 1999). She is also a designer and workshop instructor. See her website, www.sharilynmiller.com, for more information.*

introduction

My clothes have always been a little different. My mother, an accomplished seamstress, made all my outfits when I was young, letting me pick out patterns and fabrics on our annual back-to-school shopping expeditions. I'd choose a dress from one pattern, sleeves from another, a collar from a third, and two or three coordinating fabrics. My mother would put them all together in perfectly composed garments that were unlike anyone else's. The other kids, who dressed pretty much alike, always made fun of me; but I loved my clothes.

I discovered artwear in the early 1970s when I came across a book titled *Native Funk and Flash* (Scrimshaw Press, 1974), a collection of contemporary folk art from the San Francisco Bay area. Included among the furniture and jewelry were amazing garments covered with lush embroidery and appliqué. I was entranced, and I knew then that was the way I wanted to dress.

Inspired by *Native Funk and Flash*, I began embroidering on my jeans and ubiquitous workshirts. There weren't a lot of embellishments available to me back then, but I sewed on beads, sequins, and ribbon—anything I could find—and dreamed of a life in which I could wear clothes that were works of art. Then came college, marriage, and decades of trying to dress appropriately for various jobs. As a substitute teacher, I tried to wear clothes that didn't "distract from the learning environment," but I wasn't very successful: kids were always telling me, "Hey, Miss! You dress weird!"

So I finally gave up and began making the kinds of clothes you see here—clothes that reflected my life and the way I like to dress: colorful and vibrant and covered with art. I began by making old Levi's into skirts and covering them with words and images just like the pages of an art journal. Then I did the same to some dresses, and then some shirts. When I wear these clothes, I get a lot of attention. Sometimes people look away, as

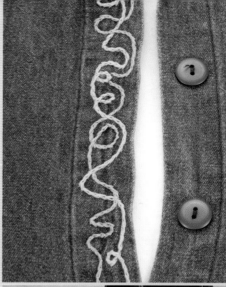

if I were walking around in my pajamas. More often, though, people will come up and ask about my clothes and read what I'm wearing. We talk about how I made them, and they always say, "Oh, I wish I could wear something like that."

And I tell them, "You can." Even if you have a dress code, there are ways to alter the clothes you wear to make them reflect your life and the things you love. If you're an artist, you owe it to yourself to put art on your clothes and show people what you do. It's not just an advertisement; it's a mission statement. Your artwear can be as subtle as a dress with a finely beaded appliqué or as flamboyant as a fully embellished journal skirt. Start with something simple and then go from there, letting the artwear on these pages inspire you as you discover how much fun it is to turn everyday items into pieces of art.

I'm lucky to have found others who love artwear, and I'm really lucky to have gotten some of my favorite artists to contribute their work to these pages. Some of them have been making clothing for decades. Others are fairly new to artwear, doing most of their work in other media; I began nagging and begging them long ago, asking for something—anything!—with their inimitable art.

Some of the artists sew on fancy sewing machines—we've got Pfaffs and Berninas and Husqevarnas here. Others, like me, are chugging along on old, basic models. My most-basic Kenmore is almost 30 years old.

So—it doesn't matter if you've sewn before or if you have a fancy machine. All that matters is that you want to make art you can wear. We've chosen projects that range from no-sew, no-stress pieces you can finish in a couple of hours (or less) to pieces that you can work on for weeks and then keep adding to for years.

techniques

Getting Started

The first thing you need is something to alter. If you've never done anything like this before, start with something simple that doesn't have long, tight legs or sleeves (they're hard to work with) or a lot of seams (hard to stamp and paint around and over). You want something that has a large expanse of fabric that's smooth and not too dark. All of this can change as you experiment; but start with something simple at first.

You can work with almost anything, as you'll see in these pages; but the soft, tightly woven fibers of muslin, old denim, and chambray are perfect for most projects. Besides being easy to stamp on or paint, they fray nicely, allowing you to cut, tear, and leave raw edges without having to worry that the whole garment will unravel. Denim and chambray are everywhere, and most thrift stores have loose-fitting jumpers made of unbleached muslin. Also, don't overlook handmade clothes—resale shops often have lots of those. If you sew or know someone who does, you can make simple vests, jumpers, skirts, or dusters that you can then alter.

As a beginner, you may want to mainly work with light-colored fabric. While the Neopaque paints from Jacquard (Resources, page 120) are terrific on dark fabric, it's easier to experiment on something that will let you see what you're doing, especially if you're going to add stitching and beading. Try using colors you love on unbleached muslin or cotton; on pale blue chambray; and on worn, faded denim.

You'll want something that fits and is comfortable—there's no sense spending a lot of time altering something that you'll never wear because you don't like the way it pulls across the shoulders or hips, or because you started with a jacket you always hated. Start with something you love to wear but that is beginning to show signs of age, or something you find at a thrift store, flea market, or garage sale. (Many of the garments in this book were purchased at thrift stores or estate sales for less than $10.) Garage sales are wonderful places to find great clothes with a tear or a couple of stains— things that make the clothes unwearable to the owner but perfect for you. Even discount stores are good places to look—Wal-Mart carries some brands of clothes that are sturdy and plain. (Check out the *Beaded Appliqué Dresses* [page 60], the *Bleached Denim Shoes* [page 58], and the *Words to Live By Jumper* [page 72]).

opposite left:
Beaded Appliqué Dresses

opposite right:
Bleached Denim Shoes

opposite bottom:
Words to Live By Jumper

You can either begin your experiments in altered clothing by practicing on pieces of fabric—trying out the ripping, tearing, stamping, and painting—or you can do as I always do and just jump in. There's very little that can't be fixed, so don't worry about mistakes. Look at the Gallery section, find something you'd like to try, and then turn to the pages in the Techniques section that tell you how to do it. Gather up your supplies. If you're going to paint or stamp, cover your work surface—large plastic lawn bags, held to the table with masking tape do the job. They're cheap and flexible and can be washed off, hung to dry, and used over and over.

Most of the altering can be done without having to use a sewing machine, but if you have one and can sew a basic seam, so much the better. If you don't have a sewing machine, don't worry: you can stitch almost everything by hand. Or you can trade with someone who does sew—have them do the machine sewing in exchange for helping them paint or embroider or add beads to their own garments.

If your garment is new, wash and dry it, omitting the fabric softener if you're going to paint, stamp, or use iron-on transfers—you don't want anything added to the fabric before you work with it.

Ripping and Tearing

Let's say your garment is almost perfect but not quite. Maybe the waistband on your jeans skirt is too tight or too high, or the dress you found for $3 has dorky little sleeves you can't stand. No problem: rip them off. Take off the waistband, remove the sleeves, cut off the hem, rip out the neckline. If you like a finished edge, you can turn it under and sew it, either on the machine or by hand, perhaps with a decorative embroidery stitch, such as the split stitch (page 45). But you don't have to—for many of the pieces shown here, raw, frayed edges are part of the design. After I began fraying the edges of my clothes, I saw a dress at a shop, made the same way and selling for a designer price. With no finished edges! So you know it's an O.K. thing to do.

You can also use a seam ripper to remove pockets, pocket flaps, and collars. *Art Doll Dress* (page 80) had a collar in its original life; I opened up the seam, took out the collar, and sewed the seam closed.

Story Dress (page 110) began as a $7 thrift shop dress with a scoop neck and little cap sleeves, which I hated. For this dress, I used scissors to cut off all the edges, but you can rip things, too—either by making a small cut and then tearing it the rest of the way or by using a seam ripper. The latter is invaluable for turning jeans into skirts: use it to rip out the inside seam from one hem up around the crotch to the other hem. Here's the way I transform old, worn-out jeans into skirts—perfect for jeans where the knees and crotch are completely worn through.

left:
On this dress, the collar was removed, and the neck seam was restitched. It was finished with a simple embroidery stitch.

above:
Here, the neckline, sleeves, and hem were all cut and allowed to fray.

TRANSFORMING JEANS INTO A SKIRT

Materials and Tools

- jeans
- seam ripper
- pins
- cutting mat or cutting board
- iron and ironing board
- sewing machine

1 Cut off the hems or, if you want the extra length, rip out the hems with the seam ripper.

2 Rip out the inside leg seams from the hem of one leg up around the crotch to the hem of the other leg.

3 Rip out the back center seam about halfway up to the waistband.

4 Rip out the front center seam to the bottom of the zipper or buttons.

5 Take the jeans outdoors and shake them vigorously to get rid of some of the loose threads. (I usually do this seam ripping outside so I won't have to clean up the threads. Birds like to use the longer pieces for building nests, so it works out well.)

6 Open the seams and press them flat. You can wash them to soften up the ripped-out seams, but it's not necessary.

7 Lay out the jeans on a flat surface, such as a kitchen floor.

8 Straighten the opened legs so the whole piece lies flat. There will be an overlap in the front and back. Pin this overlap in place, keeping the legs out straight. It's helpful to slip a cutting mat under the fabric when pinning it so everything remains completely flat.

9 Try the jeans on, checking front and back to make sure nothing puckers or bunches. If necessary, take it off and re-pin it. You may have to do this several times to get everything to lie flat, and you may have to rip out more of the back seam. Try to keep the back pockets fairly even, though—if you overlap too much, they may end up noticeably crooked. If you have to overlap enough so that the pockets do end up crooked, you can always rip them off and decorate that part of the skirt to camouflage the asymmetry.

10 Once you have the overlaps smooth in the front and back, sew them on the sewing machine. (This is one of the few things you probably won't want to do by hand.)

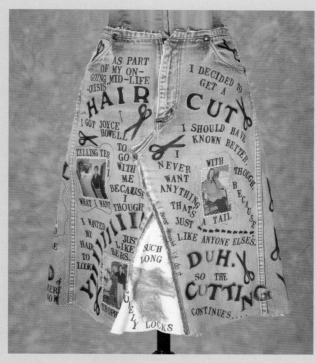

above:
Jeans can be transformed easily into skirts of any length.

11 After sewing, try the skirt on again to make sure it lies as flat as possible. When you're satisfied with it, lay it out and cut the panels for the front and back. You can use lots of different fabrics for these panels: legs from other jeans, muslin, flannel, velvet, or part of an antique quilt. It's fun to experiment. At first, you may want to stick with a fabric that's of a weight similar to the denim, so that the skirt will hold its shape better. If you want to use a thinner fabric, you might try using two layers, so it's thicker, quilting them if desired.

12 Lay the skirt out flat and insert the fabric panel inside the front opening. Pin it in place and try the skirt on to check that the panel will lie smoothly. Stitch it in place and then trim excess fabric from the seams. I always sew before I trim, just to make sure there's enough fabric for the panel.

13 Repeat step 12 with the back panel. You can sew twice to reinforce the seams, but it's not necessary. You can embroider over the stitching or couch fibers or add beads. Once you get the structural part done, you can decorate every part of the skirt.

above and right:
Attach the top of a pair of old jeans to a broomstick skirt.

MAKING A BROOMSTICK-STYLE SKIRT

If you use the legs of a pair of jeans to make the panels of the skirt on page 15, you'll have the top part of those jeans left over. Here's a fun way to make a skirt from the top part of jeans and the body of a broomstick skirt. It's also a nice way to transform an unflattering gathered-waist skirt into a more tailored style.

Materials

- broomstick skirt
- top part of a pair of jeans

Tools

- scissors
- pins
- sewing machine or needle and thread
- embroidery needle and thread

1   Cut the jeans off somewhere between the hip and the top of the thigh, depending on how you long you want the top section to be. Leave an extra $^1/_2$" (1 cm) of fabric for the seam allowance of the skirt. You can leave the back pockets on or cut them off, as long as there's a strip of denim beneath them to which the skirt can be attached. Patch any holes.

2   Put on the broomstick skirt. Put on the top of the jeans over the skirt. Adjust both pieces so the skirt gathers are evenly distributed, and attach the pieces with several pins in the front, back, and sides. Take them off, being careful not to stick yourself with the pins.

3   Lay the loosely attached pieces out on a flat surface, with a cutting mat underneath, and pin the fabric all the way around just below the elastic waist of the skirt. (Don't pin the actual elastic waist; it will eventually be trimmed off. The waist is just there to hold the gathers in place.) Use a lot of pins, as you will sew over the gathers and don't want them to bunch up all in one place.

4   Baste the skirt to the jeans. Remove the pins and try it on. If it looks the way you want it to, proceed. If not, rip out the basting and adjust it.

5   Once the skirt is basted, cut off the elastic waist of the broomstick skirt and then sew over your basting. It's a good idea to sew around twice, for reinforcement. Another option is to embroider over the stitching with thread that coordinates with the skirt. It makes the finished skirt look more like a complete piece, rather than just a piece of fabric tacked onto jeans. Add embroidery to the front and back of the denim piece and then embellish the final skirt as desired.

REMOVING THE WAISTBAND FROM JEANS AND SKIRTS

Sometimes your skirt or pair of jeans just doesn't fit right. The waistband may be too tight or too high, or you may not like the look of the belt loops. Here's a way to deal with these problems.

Although you can remove the entire waistband from a pair of jeans or a skirt, it weakens the top of the garment and interferes with the way the pockets are attached. A much better solution is to cut off just the top half of the waistband, including the top button, giving you more room and a decorative frayed edge while still leaving some support.

To cut off the waistband, find the middle of the band, the part where you can feel a slight thinning. You don't want to cut through all the layers of fabric inside the band, so cut near the middle—you can feel it with your fingers. Use the seam ripper to remove the parts of the belt loops that are still attached to the jeans.

If you want the raw edges to fray nicely, similar to those on the *Cowgirl Shrine Vest* (shown below), clip the edges and then wash the garment.

Make your cuts about ¹/₂" (1 cm) into the edge, and space them about ¹/₄" (0.5 cm) apart—spacing them wider than this will make a chunky cut, rather than a softly curled ragged edge.

above:
To remove the waistband, cut through the middle of the band and remove the belt loops with a seam ripper.

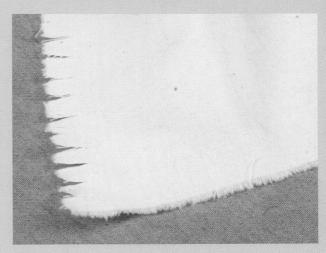

above:
To fray fabric, make ¹/₂" (1 cm) cuts about ¹/₄" (0.5 cm) apart along the edge, then machine wash.

above: **All the edges of this vest were cut and machine washed for fraying.**

Mending Techniques

How do you cover up holes in your jeans or tears in a jacket? You can use traditional fixes, such as iron-on patches, but they're often ugly and not much fun. I like to patch holes with a contrasting fabric and colorful stitching.

The most common places for tears and holes in jeans are around the pockets, in the knees, and in the crotch. The latter is taken care of when you alter jeans into skirts; the nature of its structure takes care of almost any holes or worn spots in that location. You can find jeans with unsightly holes at thrift stores.

For holes at the corners of pockets, the seam holding the pocket in place should be reinforced. This can be done on a sewing machine, sewing over and over that area to strengthen it, as is shown in the detail from the *Flea Market Silk Skirt* (page 77). Embroidery thread is a great way to reinforce old stitching, too.

right: **Patch holes with coordinating fabric. Here, velveteen was used to patch the pocket.**

PATCHING HOLES

Materials

- garment
- scrap of fabric (large enough to patch the hole)

Tools

- fabric glue stick
- scissors
- sewing machine or embroidery needle and coordinating thread

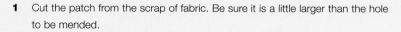

1. Cut the patch from the scrap of fabric. Be sure it is a little larger than the hole to be mended.

2. Turn the garment inside out and run the fabric glue stick around the edges of the hole.

3. Press the patch, right side down, over the hole. Press firmly to adhere glue.

4. Turn right side out and stitch around the edges, either on the sewing machine or by hand. If you use a machine, sew around the edges several times for reinforcement. If you sew it by hand, choose a sturdy stitch, such as the split stitch. (See the Split Stitch, page 45.)

On *Haircut Journal Skirt* (page 112), the belt loops had torn holes in the jeans. Rather than trying to disguise the holes, I made them part of the design, stamping a pair of scissors by them and then patching them with pieces of coordinating fabric. Your whole concept of mending will change when you don't try to hide the sewing and patching but, instead, make it a part of the design. Then it's fun, rather than a chore.

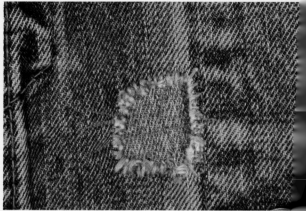

above:
Secure the patched edges with embroidery stitching in contrasting colors.

above:
Here, seed stitches were used to hold the pocket edges flat a removing the waistband.

EASY CRAZY QUILTING

Another way to disguise holes or worn fabric is to cover the area with a patchwork of fabric scraps, sort of like crazy quilting. There are many ways to do this, and you can find entire books on crazy quilt techniques. See a simple version used on the *Patchwork Bag* (below and on page 102).

Materials

- garment or fabric to be covered
- scraps of fabric in a variety of textures and colors
- fusible webbing
- embroidery floss, fibers, beads, trims

Tools

- scissors
- iron and ironing board
- needles in various sizes for floss and beads

1. Choose fabrics that coordinate with the rest of the garment and iron them to remove wrinkles.

2. Cut them into manageable pieces, a little larger than you think you'll need. Cut some into squares and some into rectangles of various sizes.

3. Iron each individual piece to fusible webbing, following the package instructions.

4. Arrange the pieces with edges overlapping. You can turn under the edges for a more finished look, or you can leave them raw.

5. When you have a pleasing arrangement, trim any that are too large or that need to be adjusted. Peel off the paper backing and iron the pieces into place, edges overlapping.

6. Sew over the overlapping edges of the pieces with embroidery floss, using a variety of stitches. (See Simple Embroidery Stitches, page 47.)

7. Add beads or trim as desired to complete the crazy quilting.

left:
A variety of fabrics, including vintage velvet and silk, was used on this crazy-quilted bag, which was embellished with embroidery and beads.

Color

After your garment fits the way you want it to, with the waistband removed or the sleeves ripped out, you'll want to consider color. Do you like the color? Would you like it better if it were different? Now's the time to make basic background changes, and there are many ways you can do this.

left:
The heel shows where the bleach solution was tested to determine the best concentration for the desired effect.

REMOVING COLOR: DISCHARGING OR BLEACHING

Many products can be used to remove color from fabric, including color remover, bleach thickener, bleach-stop (to stop the bleaching process once the desired effect is achieved), and discharge paste (paste applied with a brush for spot color removal—good for creating designs). There are also etching products (that remove fibers creating translucent areas of fabric) and whiteners, such as Fiber Etch and Optic Whitener (to get white fabric really white). You can also find black dischargeable T-shirts; unlike some black fabric that won't lose its color, these T-shirts can be bleached/discharged and then dyed. There are several good resources for these and other products. (See Resources, page 120.)

Commercial color strippers can be added to the fabric in the washing machine; however, you won't know exactly how your particular garment will react until you've tried it. There's little to lose, though, so you can give it a try. You can also add a cup of laundry bleach to a wash cycle.

For something a little more controlled, it's much easier to bleach small portions of your garment. The *Bleached Denim Shoes* (above and page 58) began life as dark navy denim. With some diluted household bleach and a foam brush, enough of the color was removed to make them look soft and faded. The color on the sole was tested (which is hidden when the shoes are worn) to determine the concentration of bleach needed for the desired look. After applying one stroke of the bleach, wait for ten minutes to check the result and then further dilute the bleach mixture with water if desired.

In addition to painting with diluted bleach, you can stamp with it by making a felt stamp pad for the bleach. Remember to clean your stamps afterwards so the bleach doesn't stay on the rubber.

No matter how you use bleach on your clothes, be sure to work in a well-ventilated area, preferably outside. Don't wear good clothes, and be sure to protect all surfaces, including your hands. To stop the bleaching process, rinse the garment and then wash in a cool water/vinegar rinse: add one cup of vinegar to a cool water wash cycle.

Some fabric artists prefer to use household cleaning gels with bleach; they are thicker substances and offer the artist more control. These will take longer to bleach the fabric (since the bleach is mixed with other ingredients), so you may need to add more bleach to the gel. Look for these gels in the cleaning section of the grocery store, where you can also find bleach pens (marketed for cleaning small areas, such as the spaces between the tiles in your bathroom). The pens are perfect for adding controlled, bleached details to garments.

There are also kits available that contain a bleaching powder you mix with water. Check your local craft store for these—they come with everything you need, and they're often marketed with coordinating trim and stencils nearby.

above:

**These shoes were originally a dark, solid denim.
Bleaching lets you get a pale, mottled look.**

top:
Spray dye was used to add color on the left. On the right, Dye-Na-Flow fabric paint was applied to dry fabric.

left:
To give the scarf a little extra color, the artist added a light wash of fabric paints.

opposite:
Color was added to the fabric patches on this vest before doing the Gocco print.

ADDING COLOR

You can add color with or without first discharging color or bleaching. Most of us have dyed T-shirts with some type of simple dye, such as Rit or Dylon, that you add to your washing machine's cycle. It's quick and easy, and all you have to remember is to run the machine through a cycle afterwards to remove any residual dye before you do a load of whites.

The problems are that simple dye will fade over time and you have little control over the outcome—you dump everything in the machine and then wait to see what comes out. More satisfying to artists is dye applied by hand, particularly the fine dyes developed for artists. The techniques used depend on the fiber content of the garment (cotton, silk, etc.), the dyes you use, and the results you want. For specific information about using fine dyes, contact Jacquard or Dharma Trading (Resources, page 120), which sell various dyes and provide excellent product support.

For simple dying without an investment in materials and time, there are a couple of easy methods for controlled dying. Two of my favorites are spray dye, which is available at craft stores (shown opposite, top left) and Dye-Na-Flow, which is actually paint with the consistency of a dye (shown opposite, top right).

The spray dye is messy and best done outdoors; however, it provides a nice speckled effect or a more solid color, depending on how heavily it's sprayed. For a lighter, more diffuse application, wet the fabric first: a slightly damp fabric will allow the dye to spread, and a really wet fabric will let the color run and bleed, which can be a nice effect. You can use a spray bottle of water in one hand and the dye sprayer in the other to dye and mist with water simultaneously.

Dye-Na-Flow is a wonderful product. It comes in thirty colors and is so much fun to play with that you will keep coming up with new excuses just to experiment. Since it's thin like a dye, it will spread after you put it on the fabric. If the fabric is damp, it will spread more. If the fabric is sopping wet (my favorite way to use it), it will spread like crazy. Use a funnel to pour the paint into squeeze bottles, and then squeeze the paint from those onto the fabric. Dilute it with water for less intense colors. The paint in the sample was applied in a single thin line onto dry fabric, with a single dot to the right of that, so you can see how it spreads, even when the fabric isn't wet. I recommend getting one of Jacquard's Exciter Packs, with tiny sample bottles of Dye-Na-Flow, to play with and test.

The *Lover's Eyes: Remembrance Vest* (left and page 106) features painted fabric Roz Stendahl used for her Print Gocco image. She used Setacolor Transparent Fabric Paints, but others will work as well. While smaller pieces of fabric are sometimes easier to work with, this artist recommends painting lengths of at least 1 yard (1 m) so that you have enough for the entire project. If you're going to stamp on the fabric, either with stamps or the Print Gocco, you'll want enough painted fabric to be able to choose where to place your images. Since you're hand painting the fabric, it will be hard to duplicate later. See the next page to learn how to create mottled fabrics in almost any color you can imagine.

TIP

Instead of scrunching the wet fabric
in tin trays, try this fun painting technique: Take the wet fabric outside in
the sun. Lay it on a plastic bag,
opened flat. Lay objects on top of it—
netting with large spaces, screens,
leaves with interesting edges—and
weight them while the fabric dries.
The image of the object will stay on
the fabric after it's dry. Finish the
process with heat setting.

PAINTING FABRIC

Materials

- closely woven bright white 100% cotton fabric
- fabric paints

Tools

- small containers and craft sticks for mixing paint colors
- tin pans or aluminum foil shaped into trays, one for each piece of fabric
- spray bottle of water
- paintbrushes—try a variety for different effects

1   Wash and dry fabric to remove the sizing. Do not add fabric softener to either
the wash cycle or the dryer.

2   Mix the paints to the desired color. Most fabric paints can be diluted with
water—the bottle should tell you how much water you can add.

3   When you have the desired colors, use the spray bottle of water to dampen
the fabric.

4   Use a brush to apply the fabric paint. You can paint layers of colors, but each
layer must be painted on, allowed to dry, and then heat set before adding the
next layer. (If you add colors at the same time, they'll blend, and if you add one
color on top of another that hasn't been heat set, the first layer will wash out
and mix with the second.) Colors painted next to each other will run and blend,
and this can be a really nice effect.

5   To create a mottled background, scrunch the painted fabric in the tin tray or
pan. Most fabric paint will wick into the peaks, leaving less color in the lower
places. Leave the pieces in this position to dry.

6   When the fabric is dry, heat set thoroughly. Allow the paint to cure for at least
two weeks before washing. (You can work with the fabric during this time, but
don't wash it.)

HEAT SETTING

Many people don't heat set properly and then wonder why the color of their painted or stamped garments fades out significantly in the first laundry cycle. All color will fade eventually, but the use of good quality fabric paints, dyes, and inks and correct heat setting will ensure that your garments will stay beautiful for a long time.

Household dryers do not get hot enough to adequately heat set paint and ink. If you have to rely on a dryer for heat setting because you have an item that can't be ironed, try to use a good commercial dryer if color permanence is a priority.

Many paints and dyes can be combined with a fixative before you use them. Check with the manufacturers for more information. Many artists find it much easier than heat setting.

Materials and Tools

- painted, dyed, or stamped fabric
- iron and ironing board
- timer

---

1 Heat the iron to the hottest setting for your fabric. Let it heat up all the way.

2 Place the fabric painted side down on the ironing board, smoothing out any wrinkles.

3 Iron each painted, dyed, or stamped section for the full amount of time listed on the label of that product.

4 Repeat for each section.

TIPS

If the instructions say, "Heat set for two to three minutes," that doesn't mean that it should take two to three minutes to iron the entire painted section. What it means is that each part that's been painted must be heated for that long at that particular temperature to set the paint. Iron small sections, keeping the iron moving back and forth over that small section for the full time, in order to heat the paint and keep it hot for long enough to make it permanent. If you've spent time and energy making artwear, it's silly not to finish the process by heat setting properly.

✳ ✳ ✳

If using an egg timer or a stop watch seems as boring to you as it does to me, try another timing method: Find a three or four-minute song on a CD you really like (and like a LOT) and select "auto repeat" on your CD player. Choosing one that lasts a little longer than the time required for heat-setting gives you time to move the fabric between replays. I heat set to Marvin Gaye's "Got to Give It Up," which is not only long enough to give me time to adjust the fabric but also gives me a reason to dance while I'm ironing.

✳ ✳ ✳

Wait as long as possible before you wash your garment—two weeks is good, three weeks is even better—giving everything time to cure. I like to paint first, then stamp, and then let everything dry for at least 48 hours. I then heat set and do all the handwork—sewing, beading, and so on. Then I wear it. By that time, it's been a couple of weeks, and everything has cured before I wash it.

✳ ✳ ✳

You might try the following method, which some artists scoff at and others recommend: Place a piece of aluminum foil over your ironing board, right side up. Place your painted fabric facedown on the foil and heat set as usual. The foil is assumed to reflect more heat back onto the fabric.

✳ ✳ ✳

Most instructions recommend using a press cloth over the fabric. It's a good idea: it will protect the fabric and keep your iron clean.

Author's Recommendations and Testing Results

Over the years, I have used and tested a wide variety of products in my artwear, and I've learned results can vary widely from one brand to another. The most important thing is to find and use products that will give the results needed for a particular piece. Higher price does not always mean higher quality and lower price doesn't always mean inferior quality. That said, I'll share information on some favorite products I have used extensively. Don't hesitate to undertake a project just because you can't find the exact product a particular artist has used. Check your local craft and art supply shops and the Internet, but then be willing to try a substitute if necessary. The goal is to experiment and have fun, and to create your own unique wearable art. Your results may surprise and please you.

PRODUCTS FOR WRITING ON FABRIC

Some of my favorite pens for writing on fabric are Staedtler Lumocolor permanent pens. They come in various widths and colors and are available at many craft stores (in the fine arts section) and art supply stores. (See Resources, page 120). I've had good results from these pens even without heat setting the ink, but I almost always heat set everything—it's just a good idea. Adirondack markers by Ranger Industries work well on some fabrics (See Resources, page 120). Some colors, like coal black, seem to be more permanent than others. Many people assume Sharpie pens will be permanent, but they don't always hold up after washing. If you want to use them, try curing for 48 hours and then thorough heat setting, just as you would with other inks and paints. Experiment with other fabric markers the same way—with curing and heat setting.

FABRIC INKS

I've tested a lot of fabric inks with mixed results. Right now, the one with which I'm most pleased is Ancient Page ink, a permanent dye-based ink that comes in dozens of colors. (See Resources, page 120.) It works well with one of my smaller, commercial alphabets that's mounted on wood and difficult to clean when used with paint. I clean these stamps with baby wipes, as recommended by Clearsnap, the manufacturer of Ancient Page. When I'm testing a new ink, I always call the company and ask for advice about heat setting, cleaning, and so on. Most companies are more than happy to provide information and suggest ways to accomplish whatever you have in mind.

IRON-ON TRANSFER SHEETS

I've also tested a lot of transfer sheets. Some brands work well and some don't; overall, the results have little relationship to how much you pay for them. The two brands I've had the most success with are Canon and Burlington. Canon is the most expensive brand I've tried, producing the clearest images and the best color. Burlington is the least expensive brand, and the results are nearly as good. Some of the brands you get in office supply stores don't work well at all, so beware. If you want to use them, test them first to make sure you can live with the results. And remember, with transfers, you want to evaluate not only the initial quality of the transfer, but its appearance after laundering (if the item is one that will require it).

ADDING WORDS AND LETTERS, PICTURES, AND PHOTOGRAPHS

This is one of the fun parts. Your garment is ready to go and now you get to add lots of personalized decoration. A lot of the pieces you'll see in this book have text and pictures on them. There are as many ways to add words and photographs as there are things you'll want to add. As you begin to decide what you want to do, here are a few things to keep in mind.

PERMANENCE AND CLEANING

If you're willing to hand wash your garment, you can add more to it than to a garment that you want to toss in the washing machine. Most techniques hold up better in gentle hand washing. If you create removable embellishments, as Lesley Riley did on her *Fragment T* (below right and page 62), you can add just about anything because it can all be removed before laundering.

COPYRIGHT ISSUES

We've all seen artwork using those ubiquitous photographs of famous people. Some of the pieces here have transfers of postcards. You can do this if you're making something just for yourself. Still, when you start thinking about copyright and the law, the best thing to do is to use your own art and your own words. If you create the drawing or take the picture or write the quote, you don't have to worry about what you create; and you can make dozens of pieces of artwear and sell them with no fear of being slapped with a lawsuit for violation of copyright. The fun of making your clothes into art is using your own artwork, thoughts, and photos on them.

above:
Two more collages, backed with Velcro and ready to wear. Because they are removed before laundering, anything can be added to them, even paper ephemera.

above:
This T-shirt features a removable collage.

This Page: Examples of stamped imagery.

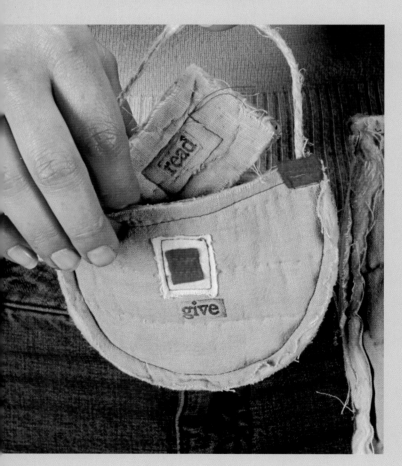

Stamping Techniques

Most of us have stamped on fabric at one time or another, with mixed results. Sometimes it turns out great, sometimes it just looks tacky, and sometimes it doesn't stay on long enough for us to decide how it looks.

You can stamp with a variety of things besides rubber stamps. For ideas, see *The Stamp Artist's Project Book,* by Sharilyn Miller. This book has ideas for stamping with everything from bubble wrap to fruit. The two most common kinds of stamps, though, are commercially made rubber stamps and hand-carved "eraser" stamps. The latter are wonderful for fabric stamping. Because you carve the images yourself, you can make the cuts deep enough to work with fabric paint, which is thicker than stamping ink and tends to clog up the lines of finely detailed stamps. There are several companies that specialize in stamps for fabric—check both the stamp section and the fabric section of your local craft store.

Many of my favorite fabric stamps are ones I've carved myself. I like to make my own images to go with specific journal skirts—chilies, a zia symbol, a voodoo doll, and a fleur-de-lis (for projects not included in this book). But the stamps I use most—all the time, on almost everything—are carved alphabet stamps. I found a font I like and carved it in two sizes. You can see it on several of my pieces, such as the *Cowgirl Shrine Vest* (page 108). It takes a while to do this, but the results are well worth it—you can toss these stamps in a sink full of soapy water and scrub them with a toothbrush over and over without having to worry that they'll be ruined. (They're thick enough that they don't need to be mounted.)

You can find much more information about stamp carving online or by checking your local stamp store for demos or classes.

CARVING STAMPS

Materials

- carving material
- images on paper
- scrap paper
- stamping ink

Tools

- cotton balls
- acetone (sold in hardware stores and found in nail polish remover)
- soft-lead pencil
- large spoon (optional)
- carving tools (Speedball Linozip Linoleum Cutter, craft knife with a #11 blade, or Dremel tool with Flex-Shaft attachment and small bits)

1   There are a variety of methods for transferring images to carving material. You can transfer photocopied images made with toner (not with inkjet ink) to the block using acetone and a cotton ball. Place the image facedown on the block and saturate the cotton ball with the acetone. Wet the back of the paper image and burnish with the back of the spoon.

   A much less toxic—and easier—method is to trace the outline of the image with a soft-lead pencil, turn the drawing facedown on the block, and burnish it with the back of the large spoon or your thumbnail until the graphite transfers to the block.

2   If you're carving an alphabet or words, remember that the images must be reversed on the carving block to appear right when they're stamped. This reversal occurs automatically when you transfer by one of the methods in Step 1.

3   Using one of the carving tools, cut away all the parts you don't want to print. Stop and test the stamp every so often to make sure you're going in the right direction. Take your time—carving can be meditative.

Left:
Eraser carving: transfer sketch to eraser, and carve away negative space with carving tools. Two finished prints are shown at left.

STAMPING WITH INK

You can stamp on fabric with ink or paint. To use ink, you must choose one that's permanent on fabric. Again, the key is testing. Here's a good testing method.

Materials

- scrap of fabric similar to garment to be stamped
- ink

Tools

- permanent marking pen
- stamp
- timer
- iron and ironing board
- washing machine and dryer

1   Using a well-inked ink pad, stamp the same image four times on scraps of fabric. Do this on two separate pieces of the fabric. Stamp the images at least 3" (7.5 cm) apart.

2   On one image (on each piece), write No Heat. Don't heat set this one. On the next, heat set for one minute and label that one with a 1. Heat set the next one for two minutes and label it 2. Do the next one for three minutes and label it 3.

3   Set one test scrap aside and let it cure for two weeks before washing it. Wash the other one immediately, just to see what happens. Compare and determine which level of fading you prefer. A faded image may be just perfect for a particular project.

right:
Scarf stamped with ink (see page 78)

STAMPING WITH fABRIC pAINT

Fabric paint and stamps can be tricky. Make sure the paint you use is either permanent or can be mixed with a fixative to be made permanent (check manufacturers). Several of the garments featured in this book use these products by Jacquard: Lumiere, Traditional Textiles, and Neopaque. These widely available paints are favored by many professional fabric artists, but please experiment with whatever fabric paints are available to you. You can achieve interesting results with many types of paint.

Some paints are transparent (Traditional Textiles, for example) and will look different on darker fabric than they will on plain muslin. Others, such as Neopaque paints, are opaque. They're great on denim, darker fabrics, or fabrics that have been painted.

Sometimes you'll want to use the paints as they come out of the jar, and sometimes you'll want to thin them slightly with water. Read the label of each product for information about thinning. You can buy un-inked ink pads and apply your paint to those, or you can make your own by cutting a square of felt the size of your stamp and using double-sided tape or fast-drying glue to adhere it to a foam plate. Apply a little of the paint with a plastic spoon and work it into the felt. Test by stamping on scrap fabric, adding more paint as needed. You'll need to add more paint to the felt regularly as you stamp.

You can also apply paint to the stamps with a brush or sponge. Apply paint with different sponges for a variety of textures when you stamp.

Remember that this isn't an exact science. All your stamped images aren't going to be perfect. You can touch up parts that didn't print by tapping on a little paint with a cotton swab, but the best approach is to revise your attitude. It's hand stamped; it's supposed to be rougher than it would be if you had the garment silk-screened. To make the edges of large letters or graphic shapes look smoother and more finished, you may wish to embroider around them. This can take some time, but it makes the letters or shapes look as if they've been appliquéd on the garment. Alternately, you can outline letters with a permanent pen, dimensional fabric paint, beads, or other embellishments.

Mix colors for a wider palette. Add glitter or metallic pigments, such as Jacquard's Pearl-Ex Pigments. Save small plastic containers with lids to use for storing custom mixes. Experiment!

left:
Stamp with fabric paint; and, when it's dry, embroider around the edges using a split stitch, as shown on the right, to highlight the letters.

USING PRINT GOCCO

The Print Gocco, familiar to artists in a variety of media, is a low-tech,
at-home silk-screening device. It is quick, requires no special chemicals
except the ink, and cleans up easily. You can use it to transfer images to
paper, cardstock, and other surfaces—and to fabric, with the use of the
Print Gocco B6 unit and the Fabric Printing unit. Roz Stendahl used
these to create her *Lover's Eyes: Remembrance Vest* (left and page 106)
and provides these instructions to help you understand what's involved
in the process.

Materials

- closely woven bright white 100% cotton (or fabric dyed or painted
  for your needs)
- toner copy of your image (not inkjet)

Tools

- **Print Gocco B6 unit**
- **Print Gocco Fabric Printing unit**

1   Insert the toner copy into the B6 unit.

2   Insert a fresh screen, a blue filter sheet, and two Gocco flash bulbs, following
    the instructions that come with the unit.

3   Close the unit. You'll see a flash inside and hear some crackling noise.

4   Open the machine and remove the newly created stencil of your artwork.

5   Leave your original paper copy in place to help in inking. Lift the clear plastic
    overlay on the top of the screen and apply the fabric ink wherever you see
    your image through the screen.

6   Allow the plastic sheet to fall back over the inked screen. Tape the two loose
    corners to the cardboard frame.

7   Take the fabric-printing handle and place its base over the clear plastic
    sheet on top of the screen. The plastic sheet will adhere to the sticky base
    of the handle.

8   Stamp on test fabric—the pressure from the handle will press the plastic-
    covered screen against the ink, squeezing it through the stencil.

9   Stamp your fabric. Allow it to dry for at least two hours—preferably overnight.
    Heat set.

ADDING WORDS AND LETTERS

Text will set your clothing apart right away. People love to read other people's clothing. People stop me all the time to read my journal skirts, such as *O, My Heart Journal Skirt* (page 104). So the first thing you want to think about is what you want other people to see. No matter how sure you are that nobody will ever read the whole thing, you'll find that someone will.

The easiest way to put text on your clothes is to write on the fabric with a permanent pen, as Lynn Whipple did on her *Art Studio Apron* (page 56). You can use fabric paint pens, gel pens, and paint markers; or you can try a variety of regular pens.

You can vary your handwriting, making your lines shorter or longer to fill available space. Or you can stamp or stencil text and then go back and jot notes in pen or marker. Think about pages in an art journal and how they might look translated to fabric.

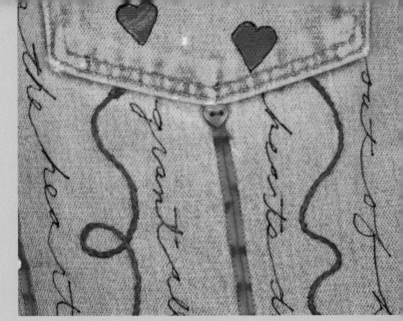

above:
This skirt will be washed a lot, so the words were written with Lumocolor pens and then heat set.

above:
Because this apron won't be laundered repeatedly, the words were written with permanent markers.

STENCILS

You can find hundreds of different stencils, many of which are letters, in all kinds of styles and sizes. These come in cardstock, plastic, and metal. You can use permanent ink or fabric paint, applying it with a brush, sponge, or dauber. Experiment on scrap fabric for even more possibilities.

above:
Geometric shapes were stenciled onto these leather shoes.

above:
**Almost any image—or words—can be
transferred to fabric.**

Image Transfers

USING IRON-ON TRANSFER SHEETS

Iron-on inkjet transfers are the most commonly available transfer sheets. They can be purchased from art and craft stores, office supply stores, copy centers, and specialty art catalogs.

There are many brands of iron-on transfer sheets on the market and they vary in price and results. Experiment with different brands to make sure the individual results are acceptable to you. Some of the least-expensive brands produce transfers that are practically indistinguishable from those created with the most-expensive brands, so don't rely on price alone to pick a sheet that will work best for your particular project. If you find a brand you like, you may be able to purchase them in bulk to save money. (See Resources, page 120.)

Follow the directions on the package for creating the images on the sheets—those are pretty basic and the same for most brands. You'll either scan words or images into your computer or create them on the computer and then print them out, reversing the image because it will reverse again when you iron it on fabric.

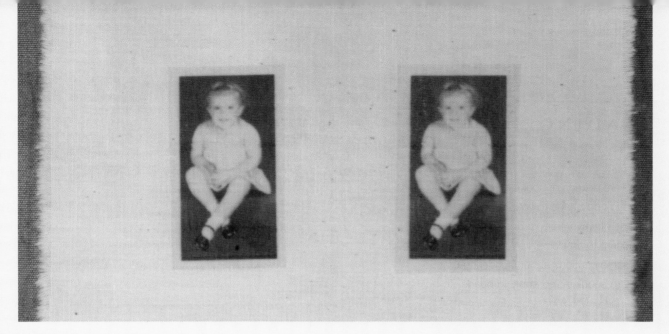

above:

The image on the left has a shiny, rubbery texture. To remove the sheen (as shown at right), cover the transferred image with waxed paper and iron over it.

ELIMINATING SHINY SURFACES FROM A FABRIC TRANSFER

Follow these instructions for getting a nice transfer that doesn't have a slick, shiny, rubbery surface. (The photo above shows two transfers: the one on the left has a rubbery surface, and the one on the right does not.) The final steps of this method will eliminate the shiny surface.

Materials

- transfer papers
- tightly woven cotton fabric
- waxed paper

Tools

- scissors
- iron and ironing board

1   Prepare your transfers according to package instructions. When the ink is dry, cut out the transfer, using sharp scissors for a clean, smooth edge—rough edges don't transfer as well.

2   Heat your iron to the highest setting for the fabric you're using.

3   Iron the fabric so that it's completely smooth.

4   Place the transfer facedown on the fabric.

5   Iron the transfer to the fabric, pressing very firmly but moving the iron so that the steam holes in the surface of the iron won't leave unheated spots on the transfers. Make sure you get all the edges and corners. Be sure to press—the transfers that don't work are usually the result of inadequate pressure. For this reason, most instructions say to use a flat surface that's sturdier than an ironing board. Don't scorch the fabric; keep the iron moving. Just like with heat setting, time your ironing. Don't skimp!

6   Let the transfer cool and then peel off the backing paper in one smooth motion. (If you're using hot peel sheets, follow the package instructions instead of this step.)

7   Lay a piece of waxed paper over the entire transfer. Iron again, but without pressing as hard this time—the pressure isn't as important as the heat at this stage.

8   Immediately peel off the waxed paper. Do not let it cool!

9   The transferred image should no longer be shiny or rubbery. You've melted the image, held in the transfer coating, into the fabric. You can repeat with a new piece of waxed paper if the image is still shiny.

10   The image will be a little stiff, but it will soften after washing.

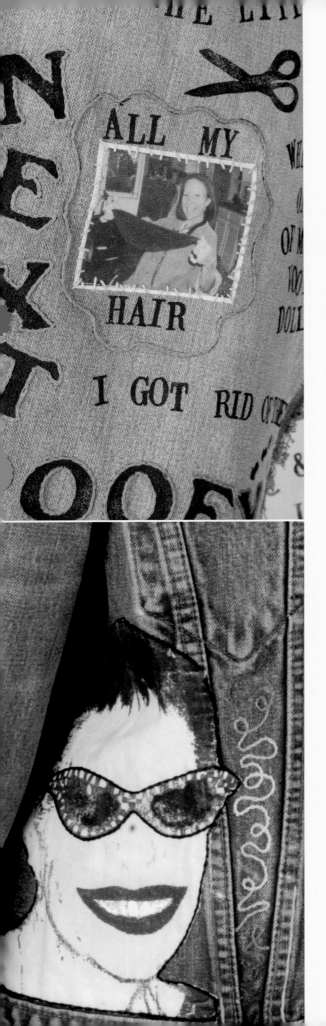

TIPS fOR TRANSfERS

Experiment with soft-lead colored pencils, soft colored chalk, oil pastels, or crayons to color black-and-white images. Color directly onto the transfer sheet before ironing the image onto fabric. Be careful not to scrape off the plastic coating of the sheet—be sure that pencil leads are not too sharp, and hold them at an angle so they won't dig into the surface. Chalks work especially well—blend them with a fine-tipped cotton swab. I used chalks to add color to the image on *Empress of the Universe* (left and page 116).

✱ ✱ ✱

There are many ways to embellish transferred images. Enhance an image with beading and embroidery. Fabric markers don't always work well, as the image makes it difficult for the markers to penetrate the fabric. Experiment anyway, though, as brands differ. Acrylic paint will adhere to the image— as seen on the *Salvaged Denim Jacket* (below and page 92), where the eyes and lips of the transfers are painted after they were ironed to fabric.

✱ ✱ ✱

Save the scraps of blank transfer paper that you cut away from your images. You can color or draw on these with crayons, soft-lead colored pencils, or oil pastels, and then iron that onto fabric, sealing in color that would otherwise wash out in the laundry. It's fun to draw colorful stick figures this way. If you can write or print backward, you can transfer letters and words.

✱ ✱ ✱

While most of your transfers will probably be created using the "best" print option on your printer and will be transferred to smooth white fabric, there are other things that are fun to try. Print the images on the "economy" setting and iron them onto lightly colored or patterned fabric for subdued, even ghostly images. The *Postcard Dress* (right and page 66) is a good example of this. I also like to do this on painted fabric as a background over which I can sew small appliqués. Try this method with pages from your journal. Cut them into smaller pieces and iron them on the collar or cuffs of a garment or on the pockets of jeans or a chambray shirt.

✱ ✱ ✱

Invariably, some transfers won't work out. The transfer will be incomplete, or parts of it will lift off, for a variety of reasons. Save it anyway—there are all kinds of things you can do with it. I made a full-sheet transfer of a photograph of my face. Part of it lifted off. I tried painting the blank spots, but that looked even worse. So I used a permanent fine-tipped pen to draw lines and curlicues all over the face, and then I embroidered those, creating a fantasy tattooed face that I really like. Never throw away a transfer—alter it, cut it up, use parts of it in a fabric collage—there's always something you can do with it. Appliqué fabric over the bad spots, paint over them, or embroider them.

opposite, top:
An example of an image transfer from a photograph.

opposite, bottom:
On this image, the lips and hair didn't transfer well, so they were painted over with acrylic paints.

right:
The postcard transfers were ironed onto the colored fabric of this dress for a muted, monochromatic look. The faces on the buttons were ironed to plain muslin so they would show up in more detail.

Some fabric artists recommend soaking the fabric in a vinegar rinse before washing. I don't do this, but it's worth trying for permanence.

※ ※ ※

To minimize fading, make sure the transfer is ironed on thoroughly, and be sure to turn the garment inside out before laundering on a short, gentle cycle. Problems result in part from the transfer rubbing against other fabric, buttons, and the like, during the wash cycle. Hand washing and hang drying will ensure the least wear.

TRANSFERRING TO SHEER FABRICS

Images can be transferred onto sheer fabric, such as organdy. *Story Dress* (below and page 110) has images on the organdy streamers and front panel overlay. You'll have to use a much cooler iron to keep from melting the fabric, but with enough pressure, you can get a good transfer. Instead of using the waxed paper method to get rid of the shiny finish, put another piece of the same fabric over the transfer, to form a sandwich. Cover both sides of the sandwich with waxed paper (to keep the transfer from sticking to the iron or ironing board cover) and iron. The image will be sandwiched between the two layers of sheer fabric. You'll need to experiment with the technique to make your particular fabric washable— hand washing is best for these sheer transfers. Be careful if you put them in the dryer—sometimes they'll curl over and stick to themselves. It's best to dry flat or hang to dry. These transfers to sheer fabric are more trouble than transfers to plain cotton, but the resulting translucent images are lovely. This dress, complete with organdy transfers, has been washed and dried in the washing machine with no problems.

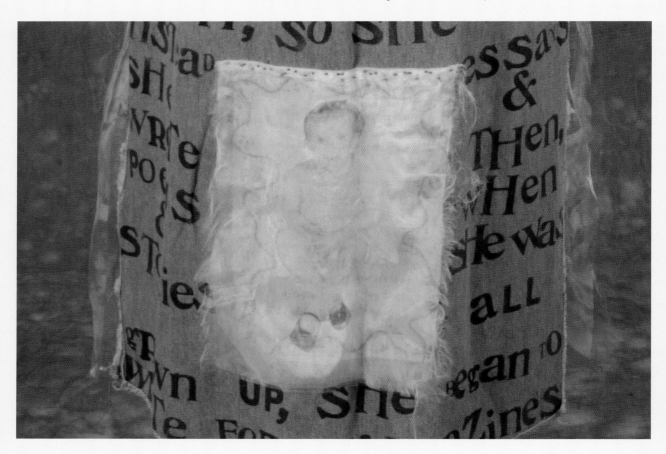

PRINTING IMAGES DIRECTLY ON FABRIC

Letters, words, picture, photographs, and graphic designs can be printed directly on fabric. Artist Keely Barham uses this technique on her *Altered People Coat* (below and page 114). Here is her method for printing images onto fabric. (She uses an Epson printer and Durabrite archival inks; unlike most inks for inkjet printers, these are permanent.)

opposite:
Here, the image was ironed onto nylon organdy so that the text, transferred to cotton, would show through.

right:
This artist uses an Epson printer with Durabrite permanent inks to print her images directly onto fabric.

INKJET FABRIC PRINTING

Materials

- tightly woven, smooth white cotton fabric (bright white fabric with a high thread count works best)
- freezer paper
- images

Tools

- paper cutter
- iron and ironing board
- computer and scanner
- inkjet printer and archival inks

1. Iron the fabric smooth.
2. Use the paper cutter to cut the freezer paper into 8 1/2" x 11" (21 cm x 28 cm) sheets.
3. Iron the shiny side of the freezer paper to the wrong side of the white fabric.
4. Trim the fabric to the size of the freezer paper.
5. Create collages or other art and scan the images into your computer.
6. To print, choose the "best" setting and the setting for heavyweight paper. Do not reverse the images.
7. Feed one sheet at a time into the printer, making sure that the fabric side will be printed.

After the ink dries, cut out the images and peel off the freezer paper backing. Iron the transfers to iron-on adhesive, such as Wonder Under, to attach to your garment. Save the freezer paper pattern—these are wonderful for masking the images. If you want to add paint to the piece later on, lay the freezer paper over its transfer to block the paint from the transfer.

If you don't have archival inkjet inks, you can prepare fabric for printing by soaking it in one of a variety of solutions that will make the inks permanent. Dharma Trading Company offers several options. (See Resources, page 120.)

Appliqué

There are many ways to appliqué one fabric onto another, and there are entire books devoted to the details.

The easiest way to attach a piece of fabric to a garment is with iron-on adhesive. There are several brands available, and they come in a variety of weights. They're easy to use, but the problem is that the bond can weaken and corners of the appliqué can begin to pull loose with repeated washings. For that reason, it's best to use the iron-on adhesive as a temporary attachment and then stitch around the edges for permanence. It's a good technique for making smooth attachments before you sew—so that the pieces don't pucker or shift as you work on them.

Permanent fabric glue is useful; but it, too, needs reinforcement on garments that will be washed over and over. Some glue will bleed through certain fabrics, so be careful when you use it for even temporary adhesion. Test your products on scraps first.

For sewn appliqués, you can choose to leave the edges of the appliqué exposed, so that they'll fray, or you can tuck them under, for a smooth look.

CREATING AN APPLIQUÉ WITH FINISHED EDGES

Materials

- smooth fabric (start with cotton for practice)
- garment
- iron-on fabric adhesive
- papers
- thick cardstock
- fabric glue stick

Tools

- scissors
- pen or fabric pencil
- spray bottle of water
- iron and ironing board
- embroidery hoop, slightly larger than image to be appliquéd (optional)
- sewing machine or needle and thread

TIPS

If you have a sewing machine that does decorative stitching, use a blanket stitch to attach the appliqué. This looks great and is a lot faster than sewing by hand.

✂ ✂ ✂

You can use embroidery thread and a split stitch (The Split Stitch, page 45) to attach the appliqué, as I did on the *Empress of the Universe Shirt* (left and page 116). The stitching will show, so choose a thread color that enhances the appliqué.

left:
Here, a split stitch was used to attach the edges of the appliqué to the shirt. It's sturdy, plus it adds a highlight color to the image.

1. If you've never done appliqué before, practice with a simple shape, such as a large circle. Draw or trace the circle on white paper. If you were drawing something more complicated, at this point you'd adjust the image until it looks the way you want it to.

2. Cut out the paper pattern and trace the image onto the cardstock. Cut out the cardstock image.

3. Place the fabric right side down on the ironing board and iron it completely smooth. Place the cardstock pattern on the wrong side of the fabric. With the pen, trace around the pattern about $1/2$" (1 cm) away from the edge, creating a $1/2$" (1 cm) margin on the fabric.

4. Cut out the fabric on the line. Place it on the ironing board, facedown, and mist the fabric with the spray bottle.

5. Place the cardstock pattern in the center of the fabric and begin to fold the margin of the fabric up over the pattern, creasing the fabric against the edges of the cardstock and ironing as you go. Take your time and do this neatly for a crisp edge and exact shape. Heat each part long enough to dry the fabric, setting the crease.

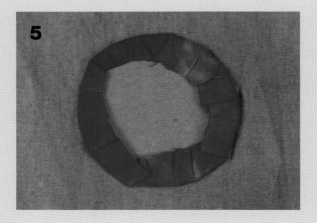

right:
A cardstock template makes it easier to turn under the edges of simple shapes for appliqué.

6. When the margin has been creased, remove the cardstock pattern. Apply fabric glue stick on the margin and press it back in place.

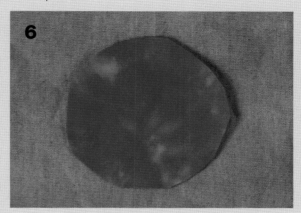

7. Lay the appliqué face up on the iron-on adhesive and iron according to package instructions. I find it easiest not to cut the adhesive to size before ironing. Cut a square of adhesive, on its backing paper, just a little larger than the circle. Place the fabric face up on the adhesive, and then put a piece of waxed paper, just a little larger than the square of adhesive, over that. The waxed paper prevents the extra margin of adhesive from sticking to the iron.

8. Peel the appliqué from the backing sheet. Trim off or fold under any threads of adhesive that may stick out around the edge. Place the appliqué face up on the garment. Pin it in place and try on the garment to adjust placement. Remove the pins and iron the appliqué to the garment, following the package instructions for heat and timing.

9. Insert the appliquéd section of the garment into an embroidery hoop slightly larger than the appliqué. Tighten without pulling or puckering the fabric.

10. Use the needle and thread to sew the edges of the appliqué in place. Use either a decorative stitch, such as a blanket stitch, or one that's hidden in the crease of the appliqué. I use a hem stitch that's completely hidden.

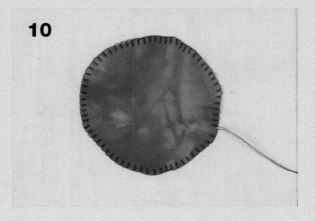

MAKING A SHRINE APPLIQUÉ

You can use appliqués to create wearable shrines, similar to the one on this *Cowgirl Shrine Vest* (opposite and page 108). There are all kinds of ways to do this; here's one easy version.

Materials

- smooth white cotton fabric, 10" x 14" (25.5 cm x 35 cm)
- slightly larger piece of colored cotton fabric
- image to go inside shrine

Tools

- embroidery needle and thread
- iron-on transfer of shrine template (page 119)
- iron and ironing board
- scissors
- colored pencils
- needle and thread

1 Copy the template on page 119, sizing it as needed to fit on a standard 8 1/2" x 11" (21 cm x 28 cm) sheet of paper.

2 Cut out the middle square of the paper. That central space will be used to create a design for the front of the doors. The two doors will open along the center (you will eventually cut the line there), and be hinged at each side. When the doors are open, the inner shrine image is revealed. Center the shrine frame over the image you want to use for the outside of the doors. If you want to add color or additional designs, add that to the paper.

3 With the shrine centered over the image that will appear on the doors, scan it into your computer, reverse it (if necessary), and then print it onto transfer paper.

4 Trim the transfer paper image around the outside border of the shrine and then iron it on muslin. Do any embellishing (stitching, beading, sequins, etc.) that you want on the outside of the shrine doors now. (You'll do this before attaching the lining of the doors, so that the lining will cover any threads.)

5 Use a fabric glue stick to hold the muslin to a slightly larger piece of cotton fabric, which will become the lining for the doors of the shrine. (Blue fabric is used for the lining on the *Cowgirl Shrine Vest*, see page 108.) The colored fabric should extend a little around the edges so the color will show.

6 Sew along all edges of the doors, then sew two parallel rows of stitches (shown on the template) down the middle, with a space between them for cutting the doors apart. This will attach the cotton lining fabric to the inside of the doors so that they'll look finished when they're open. You can also sew around the outside edges of the shrine if you wish, although that's not necessary if you're not going to embellish it further; the layers will be sewn together when you sew the shrine to the garment. Embroider the heart and lines and do any beading or embellishment you want to do before you

attach the shrine to the garment. Don't attach it yet, though—just determine where you want it to go and mark that with pins.

7 Using the rotary cutter and mat, cut the doors down the center line (between the two rows of stitching) and across the top and bottom edges. Don't cut at the "hinge" edges. Set aside.

8 Create your transfer image for the inside of the shrine and iron it on the garment.

9 Pin the outside of the shrine to your garment over the central image for the inside. Check the placement and sew in place, either by hand or machine, just inside the outside border of the shrine and along the "hinge" edges of the door.

10 After laundering, the cut edges of the shrine will fray outside the stitching lines for a softer look. The *Cowgirl Shrine Vest* was sewn completely by hand, except for attaching the lining to the doors, so this design can be applied without a machine.

TIPS

Draw your own shrine, adding lots of curlicues and decorative parts that you can embroider and bead.

✳ ✳ ✳

Fabric book pages can be created the same way—rather than having something that opens in the middle, make it open from one side, with fabric pages attached.

✳ ✳ ✳

Re-create parts of your art journal to wear on a jacket, making iron-on transfers of actual pages.

above:

**The inside of the doors of the shrine
are lined with coordinating fabric that
is visible when the shrine is opened.**

Threads and Fibers

There's no quicker or easier way to add color to fabric than with thread and fiber. There are so many different kinds of fibers available that you can't possibly experiment with them all, but you can have a lot of fun trying. The main considerations are whether they'll shrink and whether they'll fade. If you're not sure, test decorative threads and yarns by sewing them on a scrap of fabric and then running it through the laundry.

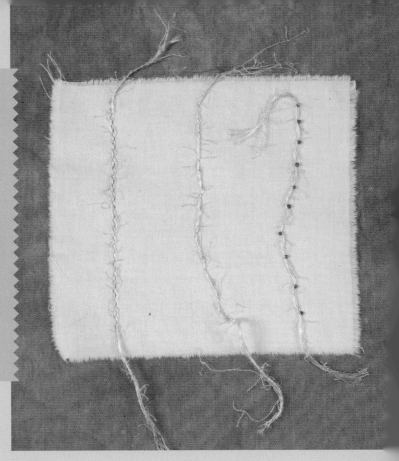

above:
The fiber on the left was couched by machine with a zigzag stitch and coordinating thread. The one in the middle was couched by hand, and the one on the right has beads added to the couching thread.

EMBROIDERY

You can do simple embroidery stitches with all kinds of threads, from standard cotton embroidery floss to hand-dyed silks, with more threads being produced all the time. (See Simple Embroidery Stitches, page 48.) The variegated hand-dyes and overdyes are stunning, and the combinations of colors are so broad that you can often find one that exactly matches the colors of paint, dye, or ink that you plan to use. If not, dye your own with dye or diluted fabric paint.

Some of the thicker threads can be more difficult to work with. Experiment with a small sampler before investing in a specialty thread for a large project.

TIPS

If you plan to do a lot of embroidery, invest in the plastic hoops, which are more stable for securing the fabric, rather than the cheap wooden ones.

COUCHING

Couching is a method of attaching thread, fiber, or ribbon to a garment with the use of another thread. You can do this by hand or with a machine, and you can incorporate beads and other decorative fibers into the couching. Lay out the fiber to be couched and either pin it or attach it temporarily using fabric glue. Then tack in place every 1/2" (1 cm) using another thread—a coordinating color, a decorative thread, or a monofilament if you want invisibility. For machine couching (the strand shown above, left), use a zigzag stitch and the satin stitch presser foot—the indentation on the under side will help keep the fiber in the middle of the stitch.

If you couch by hand (the strand shown above, middle), you can add beads as you tack the fiber, both hiding the stitch and adding embellishment (the strand shown above, right).

THE SPLIT STITCH

Materials
- fabric
- cotton floss

Tools
- embroidery needle
- embroidery hoop

1 Put the fabric in the hoop. Pull it taut, without distorting or stretching the fabric, and tighten the screw.

2 Thread the needle with approximately 18" (45 cm) of floss. A length that's too long will be more likely to tangle and knot.

3 Knot the end and come up from the underside of the fabric. Make a small stitch—for practice, you can make it 1/2" (1 cm) long. Go back to the underside.

4 Come up in the middle of the first stitch. Ideally, for six-strand floss, you'd have three strands on each side of the needle. When you're working long lines of this stitch and taking small stitches, though, it's not that noticeable, so don't worry about exact placement.

5 Keep your stitches tight without pulling or puckering the fabric. This is an incredibly sturdy stitch, and I use it exclusively when I'm mending seams, such as on the *Salvaged Denim Jacket* (left and page 92).

above:
Here, the split stitch was used both to mend the seams and to add color to a boring part of the jacket.

below:
The split stitch, used to outline the second A, is both simple and sturdy. It's also an easy introduction to embroidery.

SILK RIBBON EMBROIDERY

If you like the look of the silk ribbon roses on the *Flea Market Silk Skirt* (page 76), you might want to try silk ribbon embroidery. There are many books that give instructions, and many yarn shops offer classes. Here's how you can get started.

Materials and Tools

- silk ribbon, at least 24" (60 cm), depending on the width of the ribbon and the size of your rose
- embroidery floss
- needle with eye big enough for ribbon

1 Sew five stitches of embroidery floss to make a star as shown in A. We've used a contrasting color to show detail, but you'll choose a color that matches your ribbon.

2 Knot the end of the silk ribbon and bring it up in the middle of the star, as shown in B.

3 Begin weaving the ribbon under one thread and over the next, continuing around the star, as shown in C.

4 Continue weaving the ribbon under and over until you've covered all the embroidery floss, as shown in D.

5 Take the ribbon to the back of the fabric, hiding the stitch under the outside petal.

below, top row:
Silk ribbon roses are much easier to create than you'd think. Begin with five base stitches, and then wind the silk ribbon through them.

bottom:
A completed silk ribbon rose, created to match the silk of the broomstick skirt.

A

B

C

D

Simple Embroidery Stitches

STEM STITCH

Step 1: Bring the thread to the front of the fabric on the left end of the design line (point A). Hold down the thread with your left thumb, and insert the needle into the fabric on the design line slightly to the right (point B). Bring the tip of the needle out midway between points A and B (point C). Continue holding down the thread with your thumb as you pull the thread through to set the first stitch.

Step 2: Insert the needle into the fabric on the design line slightly to the right of point B. Bring the needle to the front again at point B (in exactly the same hole). Hold the thread down with your left thumb and pull the thread through to set the second stitch. Continue working the embroidery in this way. Try to make all the stitches about 1/8" (3 mm) in length.

To tie off, take the needle to the back at the end of the design line. Anchor the thread with three or four small loop knots.

SEED STITCH

Step 1: Bring the needle to the front of the fabric (point A). Insert the needle back into the fabric (point B) for the desired stitch length, and then bring it out at the beginning of the next stitch (point C). Seed stitches can be worked uniformly or irregularly, depending upon the effect you wish to achieve. It is best to keep them short in length and resting firmly against the ground fabric; they tend to snag when they are too long or too loose.

Step 2: To tie off, take the needle to the back on the last stitch. Anchor the thread with three or four small loop knots.

SATIN STITCH

Step 1: Backstitch around the outline of the shape.

Step 2: Fill the shape with tiny straight stitches that run perpendicular to the direction the satin stitch will be worked. This type of filling stitch is called "seeding."

Step 3: Begin at the widest part of the shape. Use an up-and-down stabbing motion for the best results. Bring the needle to the front just outside the backstitched outline (point A). Pull the needle through, and take it to the back on the opposite side (point B),

angling the needle under the outline. Continue working satin stitches very close together until half of the shape is covered.

Step 4: Begin at the widest part again to work satin stitches over the remainder of the shape. The padded satin stitch is now complete.

To tie off, take the needle to the back and carefully weave the tail through the threads on the underside of the satin-stitched shape.

BUTTONHOLE STITCH

Step 1: Bring the needle to the front of the fabric. Holding the thread down with your left thumb, insert the needle into the fabric at point A and come back out at point B. Still holding the thread down with your left thumb, pull the needle through the fabric and over the working thread.

Step 2: Repeat the step 1 motion. The stitches in the illustration are slightly separated to clarify the technique, but you should work yours close together so that no ground fabric shows through.

To tie off, take the needle to the back on the last stitch at the end of the design line. Anchor the thread with three or four small loop knots.

FRENCH KNOT

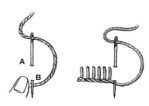

Step 1: Bring the needle to the front of the fabric at the place where the knot is to be positioned. Hold the thread taut between your left thumb and index finger approximately 1" (3 cm) away from the surface of the fabric.

Step 2: Using your left hand, wrap the thread once around the needle.

Step 3: Hold the thread taut again, and insert the point of the needle into the fabric one or two threads away from the starting point. Push the needle to the back of the fabric, all the while holding the thread down with your left thumb. Release your thumb as you pull the thread through to the back to set the French knot.

Step 4: A completed French knot. If yours resembles a "Granny's bun" hairstyle, then you've done it right! For a more prominent knot, wrap the thread twice, or even three times, in step 2.

Hardware: Grommets, Snaps, and Buttons

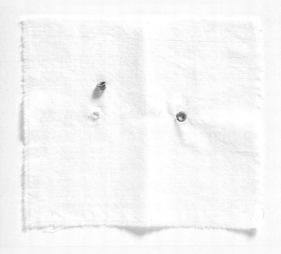

above:
Grommets are a quick and easy way to stabilize holes cut into your garment, either as purely decorative elements or as channels for threading ribbons or fibers.

TIPS

There are all kinds of studs, eyelets, and fasteners made for paper crafting. Some of these fasteners will work beautifully on fabric, depending on the thickness of your fabric and the method used to color the metal pieces. Some have paint that will wash off. Test everything first unless you're feeling adventurous.

USING GROMMETS

Call them grommets or call them eyelets—what we're talking about are those things you have on your shoes for the shoestrings. They come in all sizes and in lots of colors, and they're great for holding thread, ribbon, yarn, or string. Grommets made for clothing should be colorfast, with no paint chipping off in the laundry, but sometimes that's not the case. You may have to replace them after a while or just accept that they'll eventually be plain and metal-colored. Experiment with grommets intended for paper—they come in cool shapes, a wider variety of colors, and some of them may be colorfast in the laundry. They work great on things that don't have to be laundered often, such as a jacket.

Materials

- garment
- scrap of fabric

Tools

- hole punch or awl
- grommet setting kit
- hammer (optional—depending on what type kit you have)
- grommets

1 Test first! Determine what size hole you'll need and how much force the setting tool requires.

2 Punch holes where you want them.

3 Place the grommet in the hole and secure as directed on the kit. Some kits require you to hit the tool with a hammer. Do this on a sturdy, flat surface, such as a table protected by a board. Other kits have plierlike tools with reversible heads that allow you to set eyelets and various kinds of snaps. Look for these tools in the notions section of your fabric store.

USING SNAPS

Snaps come in many sizes, from tiny snaps to wonderfully huge ones. Some can be attached with the grommet kits discussed previously, and some are sewn on the old-fashioned way. You can use these as purely decorative elements or for their intended purpose of holding parts of the garment together. For artwear, the most useful application for snaps is to attach elements that won't go through the laundry or that are interchangeable.

You can make a collage, for instance, that contains non-launderable elements. If you sew snaps on the back of the collage, you can remove it from your garment before washing. On the *Fragment T* (right and page 62), snaps could be used instead of Velcro. For a shrine, you can use snaps to attach the image inside the doors so that you can change it each time you wear it.

above:
The decorative fragments on this T-shirt are attached with soft Velcro, but you could use snaps or buttons instead.

USING BUTTONS

Like snaps, these can be functional or purely decorative. Old mother-of-pearl buttons are one of the quickest and easiest ways to dress up an old, vintage-looking garment. A collection of colorful plastic buttons is perfect for a child's outfit; the *Animal Fair Denim Dress* (right and page 94) is a wonderful example.

You don't have to be able to make buttonholes in order to attach things to buttons. You can sew ribbon, fiber, or thin double-fold seam binding into a loop and use that as a button loop.

Making buttons out of polymer clay allows for all kinds of creative possibilities. Make them removable by attaching them with a safety pin (you can find pins created especially for this in the notions section of your fabric store) or by gluing them to a snap. Fragile buttons can be protected in the laundry by snap-on plastic button covers.

above:
Here, buttons are used as purely decorative elements, adding lots of great color to a child's party dress.

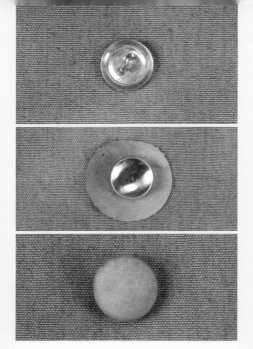

MAKING COVERED BUTTONS WITH IMAGE TRANSFERS

Covered buttons allow for many types of experimentation. You can cover them with a coordinating fabric, but it's lots more fun to cover them with iron-on transfers. Use photographs, images of flowers, or anything else you like.

Materials
- garment
- muslin
- iron-on transfers (for more on transfers, see page 34)

Tools
- button-covering kit
- iron and ironing board
- circle template
- scissors
- pencil
- needle and thread

1   Determine the button size you need. For many garments, such as the *Empress of the Universe* (page 116) shirt, you don't need to be able to undo the buttons because you can slip the garment over your head. In that case, you can use any size that looks good. Buy the button-covering kit for that button size. Once you've bought the kit, all you need to buy next time are the buttons.

2   Use the circle template to determine the size of the top of the button—not the whole button, as defined by the kit. The transfer needs to be this size; if the transfer covers the whole circle of fabric, it won't fit inside the button when you snap on the back.

3   Make your transfers (See Using Iron-on Transfer Sheets, page 34).

4   Use the template and a pencil to draw circles around the images in the size you determined in Step 2.

5   Cut out these circles and iron them on muslin, leaving enough room between them for the larger circles of muslin you'll cut.

6   Following the template on the back of the button covering kit, cut out the muslin circles for the buttons. These will be a little larger than the circle images, so center the image in the middle of the fabric circle.

7   Cover the buttons following the kit's directions. Make sure your image is cen-tered on the top of the button before snapping on the back—this takes some work but is worth it. Once you've snapped on the back, it's almost impossible to remove.

left, top:
Button-covering kits make it easy to create fabric-covered buttons for any garment.

left:
Image transfers can be used on covered buttons. Choose a larger button so the image will show.

Sequins
and Beads

Sequins aren't meant to go through the washer and dryer —most sequined garments require dry cleaning. But I've had good luck washing the pieces I've sequined, and a little testing will help you determine how color-fast your sequins are. The *O, My Heart Journal Skirt* (below and page 104) has been laundered with—so far—no ill effects. Turn the garment inside out and use a short, gentle cycle.

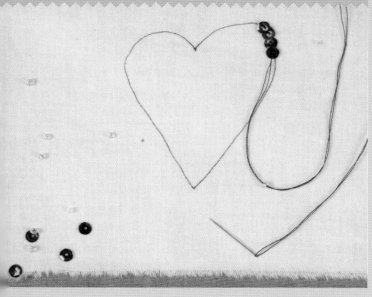

above:
Each sequin is anchored with a matching bead. Knot the thread frequently (on the back of the fabric) so if it breaks while the garment is being worn, not all the sequins will be lost.

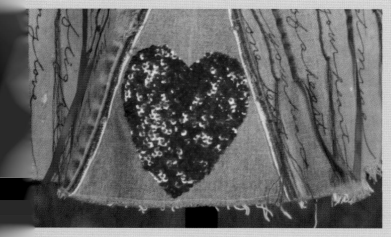

above:
This sequined and beaded heart took a lot of time to create but is stunning on the front of a faded denim jeans skirt.

USING SEQUINS

There are a couple of ways to sew on sequins. The easiest way is to sew up through one and down through the next one, but this often looks tacky, since the thread shows and sequins tend to turn themselves over. The way I like to do it is much more time-consuming, but the results are stunning.

Materials

- garment
- scrap of fabric to coordinate with your garment
- sequins
- beads to match sequins

Tools

- fabric glue stick or cool adhesive sheet
- needle and thread (small enough to go through the beads)
- embroidery hoop a little larger than your design

1   Sketch out your design on the fabric. Place the fabric in the hoop, making it taut without stretching it.

2   Start on the outside edge. Lay one sequin concave side up on the fabric. With knotted doubled thread, come up through the underside of the fabric and through the hole in the sequin.

3   Add a bead and go back down through the sequin and the fabric.

4   Bring the needle back up through the fabric at the edge of the first sequin. Add another sequin and another bead. The edge of the second sequin will lie over the first.

5   Continue around the outline, sewing each sequin overlapping the one before it. Make knots and tie off the thread frequently so that if the thread breaks, you won't loose all your sequins.

6   Continue sewing the inside of the design, always overlapping the edges of the sequins.

7   When you've sewn on all the sequins, protect the back of the stitching by cutting the scrap fabric to size and attaching it with the glue stick or cool adhesive. (It's hard to iron on fusible webbing over the lumpiness created by the sequins; experiment first.) Press the fabric in place with your fingers and whipstitch around the edges. This prevents the stitching from getting caught and pulling loose when you wear the garment.

BEADING

There are dozens of books on beading, and you can add beads to your garments in dozens of ways, from a random scatter as an accent to an elaborately beaded edging. The same cautions about laundering that apply to sequins also apply to beads. To be safe, use only colorfast beads.

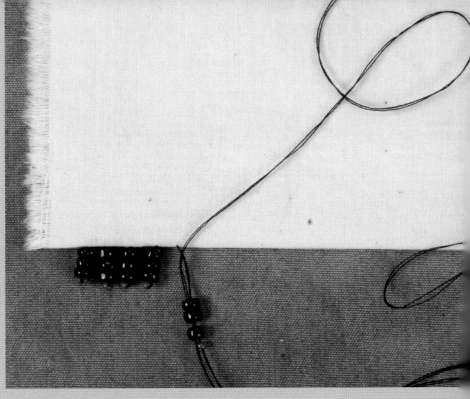

above:
Practice creating beaded fringe by sewing on the folded edge of a piece of scrap fabric. Knot frequently on the wrong side in case the thread breaks while you're wearing the garment.

TIPS

You can measure the length of fabric where you'll add fringe and make a tiny mark for each fringe to keep them evenly spaced.

✷✷✷

Vary the length of the fringes, forming a scalloped line of fringe or a staggered line.

✷✷✷

Don't make really long fringe on a garment that will get a lot of wear—it's easy to get fringe caught on things and a pain to have to repair it frequently.

✷✷✷

Seek out good beading books for further ideas. (See page 122 for recommendations.)

BEADED FRINGE

Beaded fringe looks stunning on all sorts of garments, from elegant scarves to funky denim jackets.

Materials and Tools

- garment
- beads—at least two sizes of seed beads in whatever colors you choose
- beading needle and thread

1   For beginners, it's easiest to work with the hem of a cotton garment, such as a vest or shirt. Knot the thread and come from the inside of the hem out to the bottom edge.

2   Pick up three of the larger beads with the needle, and then pick up one of the smaller beads.

3   Go back through the holes in the three larger beads. Do not go back through the smaller bead—go around it. It will serve as the anchor.

4   Go back into the fabric and knot the thread before going on to the next fringe. If the thread breaks while you're wearing the garment, you'll lose only one fringe, rather than the whole row.

5   Sew another fringe $1/16$" to $1/8$" (1.6 cm x 3 cm) from the first. Repeat along the entire length of the hem.

go to your closet!

Now that you're familiar with some simple, basic techniques for altering your clothes, it's time to get started. Don't think about it too much, and don't do too much planning. I recommend just going to your closet or drawer and finding something you once loved that you haven't worn in a while, or something that you would still wear but that could use a little art. Jump right in, doing whatever feels most comfortable. The more you try, the more ideas will come to you. Your skill will increase through your experiments.

I'd love to see photographs of what you make! (See page 126 for contact information.)

projects

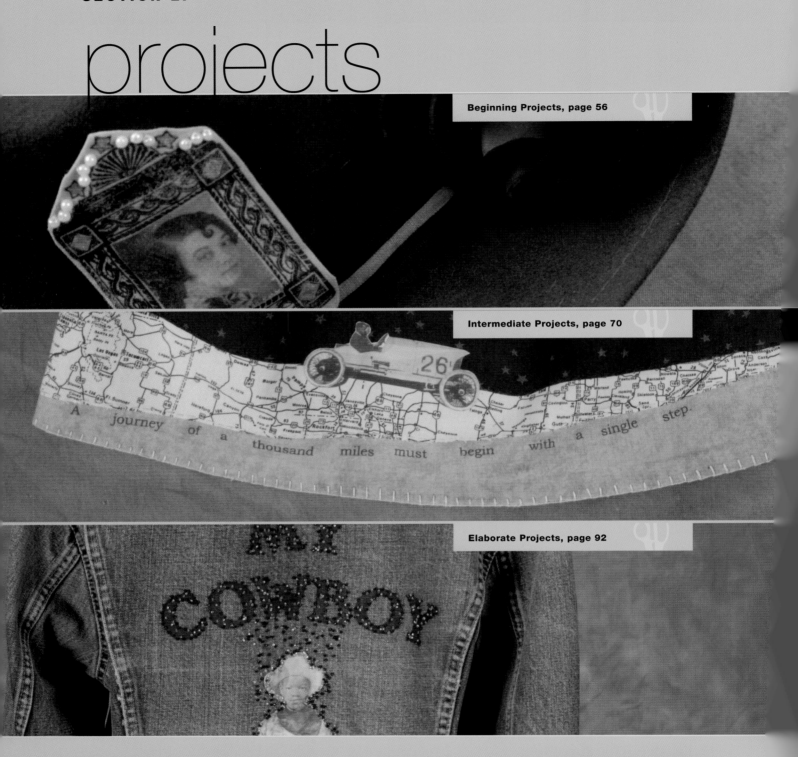

Beginning Projects, page 56

Intermediate Projects, page 70

A journey of a thousand miles must begin with a single step.

Elaborate Projects, page 92

MY COWBOY

The **Beginner Projects** will help you get started without investing a lot of time. These pieces can be completed in less than a day—often in just a couple of hours. They're fairly simple, allowing you to make something today that you can wear tomorrow.

❈ ❈ ❈

The **Intermediate Projects** require a little more time, a little more skill, or both. Still, none of them are difficult, and all of them are wonderful ways to delve a little more deeply into altered clothing.

❈ ❈ ❈

The **Elaborate Projects** are more involved. While the basic pieces aren't too complicated and don't take long to create, many of them will inspire you to create artwear with multiple layers of embellishment.

ART STUDIO APRON

BY LYNN WHIPPLE

Materials

- cotton apron, preferably with pockets
- red opaque fabric paint (featured, Neopaque opaque fabric paint)
- permanent markers, fine and bold point (featured, Sharpie pens because the apron won't be laundered)

Tools

- iron and ironing board
- paintbrush or sponge to apply dots of acrylic paint
- tiny brush for adding paint to the centers of letters
- absorbent paper cover for painting surface

TIPS

Dye the apron or paint parts of it before you add the words.

✾✾✾

If you'd like to appliqué the pocket or do other detailed work, you can remove the pocket to work on it and then sew it back on when you're finished.

✾✾✾

Add beads, fibers, and other embellishments to your apron.

This apron is the perfect project for the beginner because it lies flat, has no seams, and isn't too large and intimidating. Plus it's functional and you can enjoy it while you create more artwear!

Lynn says, "My poor old painting apron finally fell apart, so I decided to run over to the restaurant supply store and pick up a plain white chef's apron to turn into a new one. I only spent $8.95, though I'm sure you could spend much more. I wanted words on it that might inspire me when I put it on, to get those creative juices running right away. This is a really easy way to go, but there are a million more ways to decorate your studio wear, and I encourage you to make yours tell your story."

1   If your apron is new, wash and dry it to remove any sizing. Plan what you're going to write. Determine the size of your letters so you can figure how much room you'll need. It's also fun to vary the sizes so spacing won't matter as much.

2   Iron the apron to remove any wrinkles and then lay it out flat with absorbent paper under it to blot the ink that bleeds through.

3   Write the words.

4   Paint dots or swirls or other shapes to fill in the spaces. Don't forget to decorate the straps and ties.

5   Use the tiny paintbrush to fill in some of the letters. Clean brushes immediately after you're finished so the paint won't dry in them.

6   Let the painted apron dry overnight.

BLEACHED DENIM SHOES

BY RICË FREEMAN-ZACHERY

Materials
- denim shoes
- bleach
- scraps of faded denim

Tools
- rubber gloves
- plastic cup
- plastic spoon for stirring
- foam brush
- scissors
- embroidery needle and thread

Techniques
- bleaching
- embroidery

At first sight, these shoes—just $6.97—were a plain, uninspired, solid dark blue denim. Since they were so inexpensive, I took them home and bleached them. To add a little pizzazz, I dug through my denim scraps and found some faded pieces to use for the flowers. I didn't have any beads that were the right shade of blue, so I used embroidery thread and French knots to make the centers of the flowers.

1   Nothing could be simpler than this: in a small plastic cup, dilute a little bleach, about one part bleach to three or four parts water. Put on a pair of rubber gloves, get an old foam paintbrush, and take it all outside.

2   Paint the diluted bleach on the shoes. You can use two concentrations of bleach, painting some areas with a stronger concentration than others. Be careful not to get the bleach in your eyes or on your skin or clothing.

3   Leave the shoes out in the sun to dry.

4   Cut flowers from scraps of faded denim, or bleach some to match the shoes. Attach to the shoes with beads or French knots. Put the beginning and ending knots in your thread in between the flower and the shoe, rather than inside the shoe. This will keep the knot from rubbing against your foot.

TIPS

You can buy bleach pens and bleach kits at the craft store. Kits contain powder, a mixing bottle, and instructions for using stencils to add bleached designs. Try bleaching other denim clothing and bags, following the directions in the kit.

BEADED APPLIQUÉ DRESSES

BY RICË FREEMAN-ZACHERY

Materials
- cotton dress
- appliqué fabric
- fusible webbing
- beads

Tools
- scissors
- pins
- iron and ironing board
- needle and thread

Techniques
- appliqué
- beading

I bought these two dresses to wear during my long life as a substitute teacher, when I needed clothes that would blend in, rather than stick out. But even then, I couldn't bear to wear anything so plain and boring, so I altered them just a little. The coral one has an appliquéd panel of fabric leftover from a dress I'd made years earlier, accented with beads. The green one has a flower taken from a sheet that my mother used to have curtains made for one of her bedrooms—she sent all the leftover scraps to me, knowing I'd find something to do with them. This is a great way to make a practical, functional garment into something that's not exactly like all the rest, plus it's a really painless introduction to altering your clothes.

1 The appliqué here is very simple. Cut the fabric, leaving a border to turn under.

2 Turn under and press the border and iron fusible webbing to the back of the fabric.

3 Position the appliqué on the dress, pin and try on. If it's where you want it, iron it in place.

4 Stitch in place with a hidden stitch or an embroidery stitch.

5 Add beads to parts of the fabric for texture and depth. On the coral dress, I added beads randomly to some of the shapes.

6 Add beads to the border to make everything blend together. Add beads around the neckline.

For the green dress, there was no flower left whole on the scraps of fabric I wanted to use—all of them had a petal or two missing. If I'd appliquéd just a flower, following the edges exactly, the missing petals would have been obvious; so instead I left a border of the background fabric, varying its width to make the adjustment less noticeable.

❋ ❋ ❋

These dresses are cotton knit and will stretch, so you won't want to use an embroidery hoop on them when you appliqué and bead. It's sometimes helpful to work on a flat surface like a small cutting mat to keep the fabric flat without stretching it.

❋ ❋ ❋

You can scatter beads over the whole dress randomly or you can continue a pattern started on the appliqué.

❋ ❋ ❋

Attach a smaller appliqué on the back of the garment. This works well for men's shirts, which can also be appliquéd on or above the front pocket.

FRAGMENT T

BY LESLEY RILEY

Materials
- T-shirt, loose fitting
- 4" x 5" (10 cm x 13 cm) to 4" x 6" (10 cm x 15 cm) piece of fabric for base
- Velcro Soft and Flexible Sew-On Tape
- image transfers or images printed directly on fabric
- assorted scraps of fabric, trims and embellishments, beads, and charms as desired

Tools
- rubber stamp alphabet (optional)
- permanent ink (optional)
- ruler
- pins
- scissors
- sewing machine or needle and thread

TIPS

Remove the fragments before laundering.

✖ ✖ ✖

Make multiple fragments, as shown here, so that you can change them as the mood strikes.

✖ ✖ ✖

Attach Velcro to several T-shirts in various colors—you can change the shirts, change the fragments, and change the entire look.

Lesley says, "For quite some time, I had been trying to figure out how to wear my art. I have been making fragments for years and thought that they would be wonderful to wear and fun to switch around, depending on my mood or wardrobe.

"I found this softer, more flexible version of Velcro in the store and realized that would be the perfect solution—a little Velcro on the T-shirt, a little on the fragment. The small fragments are so quick and easy to make, and when I add them to my basic black T-shirt, I have a whole series of wearable art."

A really great thing about this piece is that you can remove the fragments before laundering, allowing you to attach things that can't go through the wash—bits of old jewelry, paper ephemera, photographs, and other keepsakes.

1   Cut two 4" (10 cm) lengths of each side of the Velcro.

2   Sew the two coarser pieces to the back of the base fabric, aligning the first piece a scant $\frac{1}{4}$" (0.5 cm) below the top of the fabric and the second 4" (10 cm) down from the bottom of the first.

3   Arrange the transfers, scraps, trims, and other embellishments on the front of the base fabric, pinning in place and adjusting as necessary.

4   When you're pleased with the arrangement, sew in place, using whatever kind of stitching appeals to you.

5   Try on the T-shirt and find a good location for the Velcro, avoiding obvious problem areas. Insert pins to mark placement.

6   Remove the T-shirt and sew the softer of the two 4" (10 cm) pieces of Velcro to the shirt—sew the slightly stiffer pieces onto the fragment.

7   Measure 4" (10 cm) down from the bottom edge of the first piece and sew the second piece in place. You might want to check placement first by attaching the completed fragment to the top piece of Velcro and to make sure the bottom piece will line up. This will prevent puckering.

AUTUMN LEAF SANDALS

BY RICË FREEMAN-ZACHERY

Materials
- leather shoes
- fabric paint (featured, Lumiere)

Tools
- old toothbrush
- foam brush
- stamps
- heat tool

Techniques
- stamping with fabric paint

I have more than a dozen pairs of leather sandals and I love them. They're comfortable, and they keep coming back in style; but they're not always colorful. I thought they needed a little jazzing up, so I got out my Lumiere paints. You can make your shoes any color you want and then add art.

1. Clean your shoes to remove loose dirt and anything on the leather that might prevent the paint from adhering to it. Dry scrubbing with an old toothbrush works well, but if you have to use water, let the leather dry thoroughly before stamping.

2. Use a foam brush to apply a very thin coat of paint to the stamps, and stamp the shoes. I used two stamps here—a commercial rubber stamp and a foam stamp. Both will slide on the leather as you stamp, so find a stable surface for your shoe. I unbuckle mine and put them over my leg to hold them steady. Stamp part of the shoe and then let that dry before stamping the next part.

3. Stamp the fern in metallic russet and let it dry completely. Stamp the spray of smaller leaves in metallic olive green. Let everything dry for 48 hours, and then heat set the paint with the heat tool. You want to heat the paint enough to set it but not enough to damage the shoe, especially the adhesive and rubber on the sole. Move the tool continuously, rather than concentrating too long on one spot.

TIPS

You can sponge on different colors of paint for an abstract effect. I swirled in metallic purple, green, and gold on a pair of Mardi Gras shoes.

❅ ❅ ❅

You can paint the entire shoe and then stamp over it with different colors when that background has dried.

❅ ❅ ❅

Use a spray sealant to protect the paint if you're worried about permanence.

POSTCARD DRESS

BY RICË FREEMAN-ZACHERY

Materials
- cotton dress
- iron-on transfers (you can take your photos to a copy shop to have this done or make them yourself with your computer, scanner, inkjet printer, and transfer paper)
- white paper
- unbleached muslin

Tools
- scissors
- iron and ironing board
- pins
- button covering kit

Techniques
- image transfers
- buttons

This is a really simple use of iron-on transfers. The transfers are transparent, so they'll show up much differently on colored fabric than on white cotton or muslin. For this dress, I wanted an old, stained look to go with the images of old postcards, so I ironed the transfers directly onto the dress, rather than ironing them on muslin and appliquéing them. The buttons are made from a button kit, with the images transferred to muslin. Someday I may do more to this dress, with text and maybe some couched fibers, but for now I like the simplicity of the pale, barely visible transfers.

1. Create the transfers. (See Image Transfers, page 34.) Transfer the small images to muslin.

2. Choose a button-covering kit. If the dress will slip over your head while it's buttoned, you can have any size buttons, just sewing them in place over the buttonholes. Cover the buttons.

3. Print the images to be used on the dress onto plain paper to use as patterns to determine placement.

4. Iron the transfers directly onto the dress fabric.

5. Sew on the buttons. If you won't be using them as actual buttons, and if they won't stay upright, you can glue them in place after sewing. Use a permanent fabric glue, such as O.K. To Wash It or Fabri-Tac.

EMBELLISHED HAT

BY RICË FREEMAN-ZACHERY

Materials
- hat
- iron-on transfers (you can take your photos to a copy shop to have this done or make them yourself with your computer, scanner, inkjet printer, and transfer paper)
- beads
- silk ribbon
- velvet flower pin
- fabric glue stick
- waxed paper

Tools
- iron and ironing board
- beading needle and thread

Techniques
- image transfers
- beading

I've had a couple of these men's felt hats, bought on sale, hanging around the house for years. They were dull and not much fun to wear, so I decided to make them a little snazzier, just in case I need a fancy hat. You could make a shrine on the front of the hat, with fabric doors that open. (See Making a Shrine Appliqué, page 42.) Or try adding a whole series of transfers, perhaps of Loteria cards sized to fit your hat. You can find hats at estate sales; if they're a little dirty, have them cleaned before working with them.

1 Make a transfer onto a piece of muslin, adjusting the size to fit the front of the hat.

2 Fold the edges under and press them in place, making sure to cover the transfer with a piece of waxed paper before pressing. Set aside.

3 Use fabric glue to attach silk ribbon over the hatband. Add beads if desired.

4 Attach the transfer to the front of the hat with fabric glue, beads, or stitched tacks. I used a few invisible tacks and then added some pearl beads.

5 Add a velvet flower pin (I found this old one at an estate sale and just pinned it to the hatband).

TIPS

Add beading to your hat, or attach streamers of coordinating silk ribbon.

※ ※ ※

Add soft netting to lightly cover the top part of your face for a romantic look. If you can't find appropriate netting at the fabric store, salvage some from hats at estate sales and flea markets.

※ ※ ※

Hats that are too battered to be worn can provide you with old flowers, pieces of ribbon, netting, and beads—and, sometimes, tiny feathered birds.

BYZANTINE T-SHIRT DRESS

BY LAURIE MIKA

Materials
- cotton T-shirt
- 2 yards (2 m) of rayon, printed or plain
- fabric paint in colors to match rayon
- fabric markers (featured, Marvy Markers)
- fabric glues and foils (featured, Jones Tones foiling glue)
- polymer clay or other decorative buttons

Tools
- cardboard (or shirt board)
- sponges
- paintbrushes
- yardstick
- pins
- iron and ironing board
- sewing machine

Techniques
- painting fabric
- heat setting

Laurie has traveled extensively throughout the world, capturing images, patterns, and colors that inspire her one-of-a-kind garments. For these dresses, she began with a T-shirt that she dyed and altered, transforming it from a functional-but-uninspired shirt to a gorgeous dress that's as fun to wear as it is comfortable.

1 Insert the cardboard into the T-shirt to keep the paint from bleeding through.

2 Use the fabric markers and the yardstick to draw outlines of geometric forms on the T-shirt.

3 Use metallic gold fabric paint and the sponges to sponge a design on the T-shirts, using the outlines as a guide.

4 Use fabric paints in various colors to fill in the shapes, applying with the paintbrushes.

5 Allow the paint to dry for 48 hours before heat setting.

6 Trace over the marker lines with foiling glue and allow this to dry.

7 Following the foiling directions on the package, adhere the foil to the dried glue.

8 On the sewing machine, run a gathering stitch through the 2 yards (2 m) of fabric. Adjust the gathers to fit the bottom of the T-shirt, then pin and stitch in place, right sides together. Hem the bottom edge.

TIPS

If you don't use printed fabric, paint the skirt fabric to match the designs on the T-shirt.

✦ ✦ ✦

On scraps of white fabric, paint shapes to match those on the T-shirt and appliqué them to the skirt. (See Appliqué, page 40.)

✦ ✦ ✦

Make your own polymer clay buttons or buy some from a polymer clay artist. You can also use mismatched buttons in colors that coordinate with your dress.

✦ ✦ ✦

Buy or make a dress clip to attach to the back of the dress so that it's adjustable for all sizes. Look for these at fabric stores, in the notions section.

WORDS TO LIVE BY JUMPER

BY RICË FREEMAN-ZACHERY

Materials
- denim jumper
- iron-on transfers (you can take your text to a copy shop to have this done or make them yourself with your computer, scanner, inkjet printer, and transfer paper)
- fabric glue stick
- double-fold bias tape
- beads

Tools
- scissors
- pins
- iron and ironing board
- embroidery needle and thread
- beading needle
- sewing machine or needle and thread

Techniques
- image transfers
- appliqué
- beading

This is a large denim jumper from a discount store. I started working on it because the straps wouldn't stay where I wanted them. I sewed on beads to keep the metal parts from sliding up and down; I used yellow-gold beads that matched the thread in the seams—that color they use on jeans—and liked the results so much that I kept going. I'm planning more—maybe covering the bottom with words, too.

1   Type your favorite words or phrases on your computer, in a font you like. Print out a test page on regular paper. Cut the words apart and see how they'll look on your garment, adjusting the size of the font and printing a new sheet as necessary. Use these words when determining the width of bias tape you'll need.

2   Iron the tape. Print the words onto iron-on transfer paper, making sure to reverse the words when you print.

3   Cut the words apart, leaving a border around each word. I cut mine the size of the bias tape so that the transfers would keep the cut ends of the tape from fraying—I didn't turn under the ends of the tape.

4   Iron the words onto the tape and then trim the tape to size. Arrange the words on the garment, moving them around to fill the space. I had to keep adding more words to make it look fuller.

5   Hold the words in place with a bit of fabric glue stick. This way they'll stay in place so you'll remember where you wanted them all to go.

6   Sew the words in place with beads.

7   Iron the title on muslin or fabric the same color as the bias tape. Turn under the edges and appliqué, adding beads as desired.

TIPS

Use words that make up a poem or a story on your jumper.

✖ ✖ ✖

If you don't want to sew the tape into place, use heavy-duty iron-on adhesive on the back and then make a tacking stitch in each end for security.

ASIAN DENIM DRESS AND PURSE

BY JENNIFER CRUTCHER

Materials

for the dress:

- denim dress
- scraps of colored cotton fabric
- iron-on transfers of face and fortunes from fortune cookies
- decorative trim
- all-purpose thread, black and red
- iron-on fabric adhesive (featured, Wonderunder)
- ½ yard (0.5 m) black cord
- permanent fabric glue (featured, Fabri-Tac)
- decorative buttons

for the purse:

- small red Chinese food container (available from rubber stamp stores)
- ½ yard (0.5 m) black cording
- fortunes from fortune cookies
- Xyron machine or other adhesive
- four black eyelets

Tools

- black permanent fabric marker
- scissors
- iron and ironing board
- sewing machine or needle and thread

Techniques

- image transfers
- appliqué
- embroidery

This dress and purse are a great way to use all those fortune cookie sayings you've been collecting. Print them out and transfer them to fabric, and you've got an ensemble sure to bring good luck!

Dress

1 Make iron-on transfers of faces and fortunes and iron them on white cotton fabric.

2 Cut out the faces and fortunes and apply the iron-on fabric adhesive to these and to the back of the scrap fabric. When you iron the fabric transfers to the iron-on adhesive, make sure you protect the transferred image with waxed paper to keep it from sticking to the iron or the ironing board.

3 Cut out bodies, hats, and feet from the prepared scrap fabric.

4 With the fabric marker, draw thongs on the shoes.

5 Iron faces, bodies, and feet in place. There are five people on this dress; you may need more or fewer, depending on the size of the people and the size of the dress.

6 Before ironing on the hats, cut a piece of black cord for each one. Knot one end and slip the other end under the hat before ironing the hat in place.

7 Iron fortunes in place on the bodice.

8 Topstitch around all the appliquéd pieces, either by hand or machine, using red and black thread. You can match the colors or contrast them (red thread on the black parts and vice versa).

9 Apply a bead of the fabric glue along the black cord and press it in place around the mid-section of the dress. Tuck the ends inside and whipstitch to secure.

10 Remove existing buttons and replace with decorative ones.

Purse

1 Remove the wire handle from the Chinese food container.

2 Use the hole punch to punch larger holes where the wire was inserted. Use the eyelet setter to set black eyelets in the holes.

3 Open the container and lay it flat.

4 Use a Xyron machine (or other sturdy method of adhesive) to prepare the fortunes. Adhere them in place.

5 Refold the container and run black cord through the holes, knotting each end.

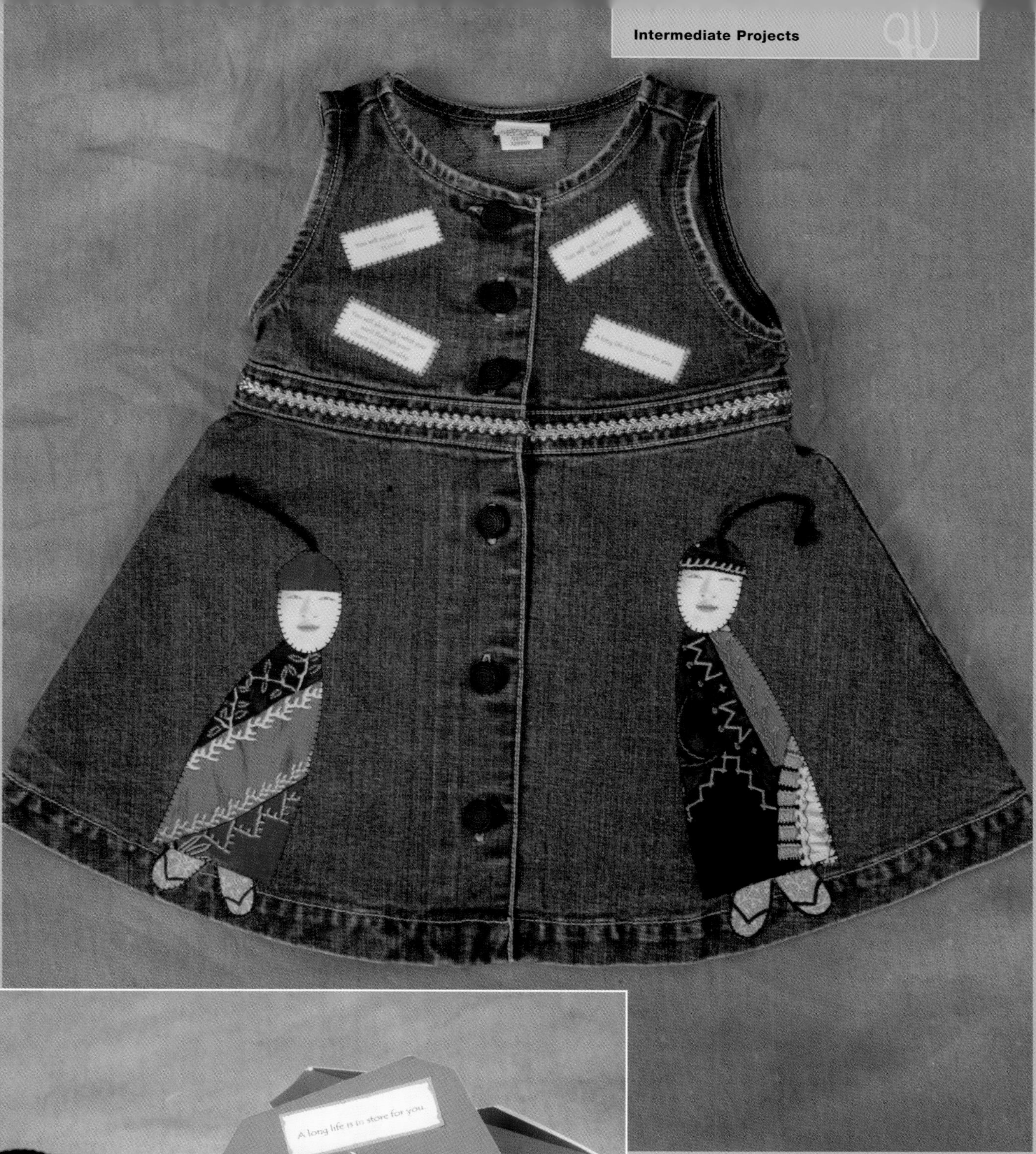

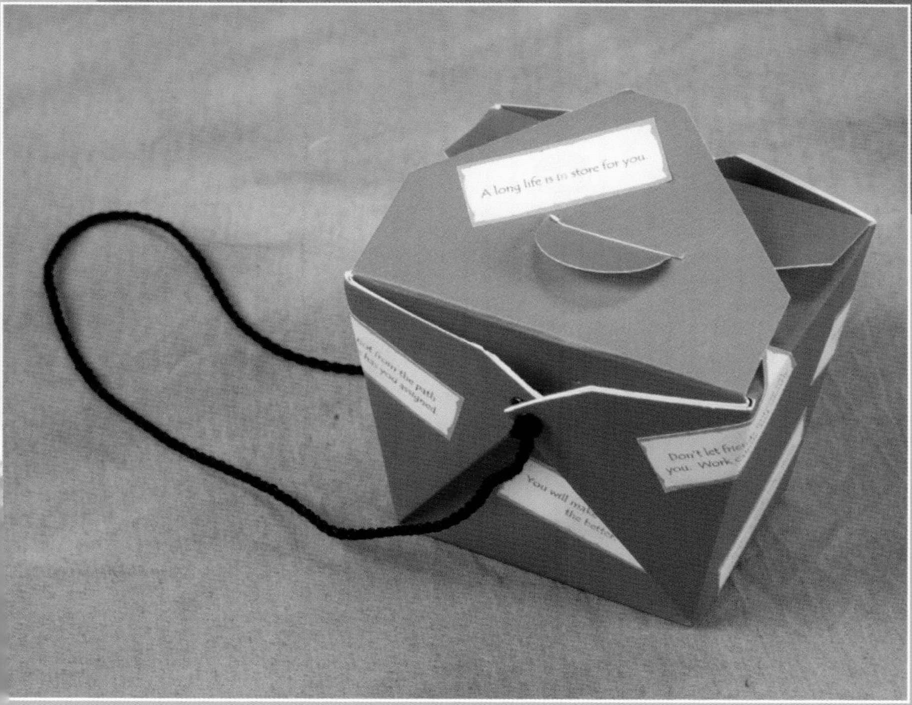

TIPS

Make fabric transfer buttons with smaller versions of the faces.

Add faces to the little purse.

FLEA MARKET SILK SKIRT

BY RICË FREEMAN-ZACHERY

Materials

- silk broomstick skirt
- top part of a pair of jeans
- scrap of fabric to patch holes
- silk ribbon in various widths and coordinating colors
- fabric glue stick
- beads

Tools

- scissors
- pins
- embroidery needle and thread
- beading needle
- sewing machine or needle and thread

Techniques

- ripping and tearing
- mending
- transforming jeans into a skirt
- embroidery

This skirt began its life as a pair of jeans and a silk broomstick skirt—one of those skirts that were so popular years ago but that aren't very flattering on anyone. I found the skirt at the flea market in Santa Fe, where a woman sold it to me for $10 from the back of her truck. I didn't notice that I'd left the skirt too long until I tried it on. (This is why it's good to try things on at every step of the way!) I'd recently seen some dresses that had little gathers randomly scattered over them, and I thought I could adapt this technique to raise the hem of the skirt. The silk ribbon embroidery roses were added to make the jeans and skirt blend together.

1   Attach the body of the skirt to the top of the jeans. (See page 16 for details.)

2   To shorten parts of the skirt, apply fabric glue stick to a length of silk ribbon and lay it on the skirt, pressing in place with your fingers. Knot a coordinating piece of embroidery thread and sew a running stitch through the center length of the ribbon. Pull the end of the thread to draw up the ribbon, and then knot the thread. You can add beads or leave the ends of the threads dangling or even make tiny tassels by adding more thread. Place these wherever you want to draw up the length a little or just add some color and detail.

3   Add silk ribbon embroidery roses to denim. You'll need a yard or more of ribbon, depending on how full you want the roses to be. (See Silk Ribbon Embroidery, page 46.)

TIPS

Add beads to both the jeans top and the skirt itself. I didn't add much to the silk on the skirt because I didn't want to weigh it down and make it too heavy to flow; but beading, appliqués, or couching are terrific additions to cotton skirts.

❋ ❋ ❋

Add more embellishment to the denim part of the skirt. If you have extra fabric from the broomstick skirt, make patches or appliqués from that.

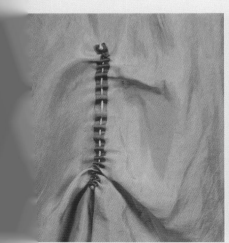

STAMPED SILK SCARF

BY LENNA ANDREWS FOSTER

Materials

- silk scarf
- scrap of silk
- fabric paint (featured, Jacquard's Dye-Na-Flow, Textile, and Lumiere paints)
- ink pads (featured, Fabrico by Tsukineko, black, chocolate, burgundy, and midnight blue)
- lace or trim

Tools

- foam brushes or sponge wedges
- small brushes for details
- thin plastic gloves (optional)
- rubber stamps
- freezer paper
- heat gun (optional)
- empty spray bottles for paint
- empty plastic containers
- iron and ironing board
- sewing machine or needle and thread

Techniques

- stamping with fabric paint
- painting fabric
- heat setting

TIPS

Try metallic gold Lumiere paint along the edges of the scarf.

✷ ✷ ✷

Sew on tiny beads to highlight some of the images.

✷ ✷ ✷

Sew the stamped scarf to a backing fabric, such as coordinating silk dupioni, to add more body.

Lenna explains, "This was a plain white silk scarf in another life. I enjoy stamping on fabric, and this type of scarf is the perfect canvas for detailed stamps. Stamping on silk is very easy to do with a Fabrico Ink Pad; the images come out wonderfully crisp. For a bit more punch, I added color to the scarf with a light wash of fabric paints."

1 Wash and dry the silk scarf and the scrap of silk. Do not use fabric softener in the washer or dryer. Although directions usually say to wash silk by hand, you can wash most silk pieces in the washing machine and dry them in the dryer.

2 Iron the scrap of silk and the scarf to freezer paper.

3 Test each stamp image on the scrap silk to determine if you need to re-ink your stamp pad.

4 Stamp the images on the scarf.

5 Allow the stamped images to dry and then heat set.

6 Add paint to the images as desired, using the fabric paints and a small brush. If you use a regular textile paint, thin it with water—about 50/50. If you use Dye-Na-Flow or a silk paint, diluting isn't necessary. Alternately, you can mix paint and water in a spray bottle to spray color on the scarf.

7 Allow the paint to dry before heat setting again.

8 Add trim or lace by hand or with sewing machine.

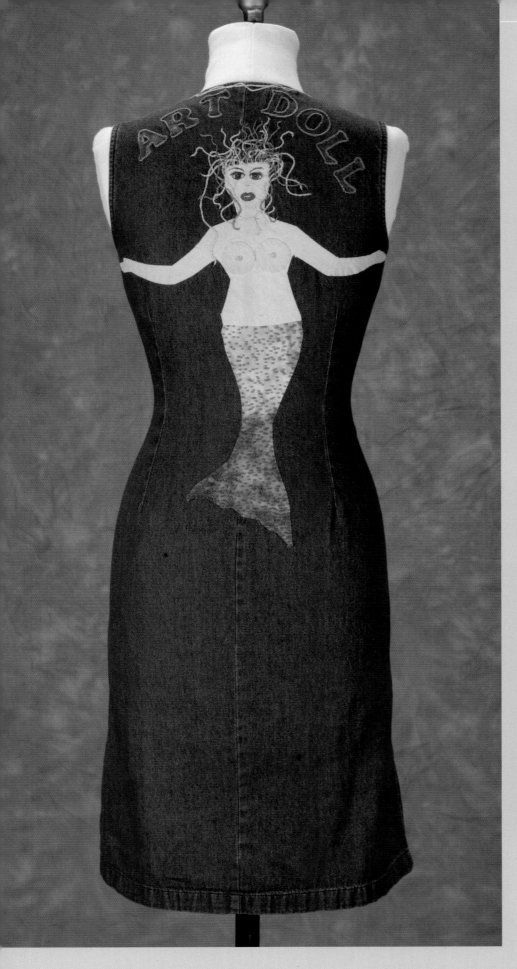

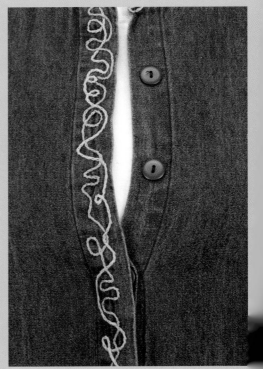

ART DOLL DRESS

BY RICË fREEMAN-ZACHERY

Materials
- cotton dress
- fabric paint (featured, Lumiere paint)
- paper
- cotton fabric for appliqué
- fusible webbing
- embroidery thread
- covered buttons
- beads

Tools
- pencil
- scissors
- pins
- stamps
- button covering kit
- foam brush for applying paint to stamps
- permanent fabric markers
- iron and ironing board
- embroidery needle
- beading needle
- sewing machine or needle and thread

Techniques
- ripping and tearing
- mending
- stamping with fabric paint
- embroidery
- appliqué
- beading
- couching
- buttons
- heat setting

From 1999–2001, I participated in a collaborative doll-making project that resulted in a book called *The Art Doll Chronicles* (See Further Reading, page 122.) It was a lot of fun when the book came out, and I wanted to do something to celebrate. On this inexpensive dress, I appliquéd a doll that looked like what I'd first imagined for the mermaid I contributed to the project (even though she looks nothing like the doll we eventually created).

1   Prepare the dress, making any alterations needed. On this one, I used a seam ripper to open up the seam holding the collar in place. I removed the collar and re-stitched the seam with a split stitch and coordinating embroidery thread. (See The Split Stitch, page 45.)

2   Stamp the letters. (Lumiere pearl violet paint was used in the sample.) Let the paint dry for 48 hours before heat setting. Heat set the paint before you embroider the letters or add beads; you can stitch the other parts of the garment once the paint is dry to the touch and while it continues to cure.

3   Make your appliqué pattern on paper, adjusting the size to fit the back of the dress, and then transfer the pieces to the fabrics. Sew it all together and get it ready to attach to the dress. (Be sure to pin the appliqué in place first and try the dress on. You want to make sure everything works and doesn't call attention to any parts of your body where you don't want it.) Draw her face with permanent fabric markers or use one of the other ideas in the Tips for this project.

4   Attach the appliqué for stitching. Use fabric glue stick, fusible webbing, or just pins—whatever works best for you.

5   You can sew the appliqué with an embroidery stitch, as I did on *Empress of the Universe* (page 116), or you can use an invisible stitch with regular thread, as I did here. A blanket stitch is another attractive option.

6   Add as many beads and embellishments as you desire. Embroider the doll's hair using the split stitch, or use couched fibers for a looser, fuzzy effect.

TIPS

While this art doll is anatomically correct, you might want to give yours a bra made of seashells or undersea flowers.

※※※

Her face is drawn on with fabric markers, but you could appliqué a face, use a photo transfer, or use three-dimensional elements, such as doll eyes, instead.

JOURNEYS DRESS

BY JENNIFER CRUTCHER

Materials
- denim overall dress
- printed specialty fabrics: map fabric, blue star fabric
- yellow cotton fabric
- white cotton fabric
- tan or tea-dyed cotton fabric
- iron-on fabric adhesive (featured, Stitch Witchery)
- anti-fray adhesive (featured, Fray Block)
- embroidery thread to match fabrics (natural and blue)
- iron-on transfers of images of old cars, passport, and computer-generated words
- tissue paper

Tools
- scissors
- measuring tape
- iron and ironing board
- sewing machine or needle and embroidery thread

Techniques
- image transfers
- appliqué
- embroidery

Jennifer collects quotes to use in her artwork and likes to find images and fabrics that work with specific words. The dress here was a resale shop find, and the little hanging pocket was perfect for one of her wonderful tiny cloth books. She had old-looking fabrics that went with her imagined theme of a long-ago road trip, and map fabric added the perfect background. She recommends using old photographs of family members to give the garment special meaning.

1 Measure around the hem of the dress and make a tissue paper pattern.

2 Use this pattern to cut the fabrics, allowing for a slight overlap.

3 Run a small bead of the anti-fray adhesive along the edge of each fabric and allow it to dry.

4 Iron each piece of fabric on the iron-on adhesive and then on the dress.

5 Prepare iron-on transfers of the words and of the images of the cars and the passport (both the cover and the inside pages).

6 Iron the transfers of the cars onto white cotton fabric. Cut out the images and iron them on the adhesive and then onto the fabric of the dress.

7 Iron the transfers of the words directly onto the fabric and onto the top of the dress (Journeys) and the pocket (Passeporte).

8 Create the passport. Iron the transfers on the tan or tea-dyed fabric. Iron the inside pages side by side onto another piece of fabric. Cut these out and use the iron-on adhesive to iron them back-to-back so that they form a book. Trim the edges and fold in the center. Iron to form a crease so the book will stay closed.

9 Finish the dress and book by embroidering a blanket stitch along the edges of the book and the bottom of the dress. Use a basic running stitch on all the other edges of the dress fabric.

TIPS

Add more embroidery to embellish the dress.

❋ ❋ ❋

For added washability, stitch around the car images by hand or with a sewing machine.

❋ ❋ ❋

Add beads to create stars in the sky above the cars.

❋ ❋ ❋

Sew tiny ribbons or beads to the passport.

❋ ❋ ❋

Sew a snap to the passport and the inside of the pocket so it can be snapped in place.

COLLAGED LEATHER SHOES

BY LINDA WOODS

Materials

- leather shoes
- white gesso (featured, Golden brand)
- matte medium (featured, Golden Matte Medium)
- acrylic paints
- photocopied ephemera (copies of photographs, postcards, tickets, etc.)
- decorative paper (wrapping paper, tissue paper)
- computer-generated text
- glaze (featured, Judikins Diamond Glaze)
- tissue paper

Tools

- paintbrushes
- stencil of geometric shapes (used for the diamond patterns)

Techniques

- painting

Linda travels all over the world teaching, making art, and gathering ideas. These shoes are perfect not only for capturing memories of a favorite trip but for introducing yourself to people you meet along the way—who could resist asking about shoes like these?

1 Stuff the shoes with wadded-up tissue paper so they'll hold their shape while you work with them.

2 Paint the surface to be collaged with a thin coat of gesso. Allow this to dry completely.

3 Paint the base surface and allow it to dry. Use more than one color if desired, or paint each shoe a coordinating color.

4 Experiment with the text, paper, and ephemera to find the best arrangement. Make a mental note or, better yet, a sketch to remind you where to put everything.

5 Use matte medium to adhere the papers to the shoes, pressing out air bubbles with your fingers as you work.

6 Let this dry completely and then stencil geometric shapes, using a brush to apply the paint. Be careful not to let paint seep under the stencil. Let the paint dry completely.

7 Apply one or two coats of the glaze, letting the shoes dry thoroughly between coats. Allow the shoes to dry completely before you wear them.

TIPS

Use a sturdy beading thread to sew on beads.

※ ※

Attach grommets, using an awl to punch holes. (See Using Grommets, page 48.) Thread decorative fibers or colored wire through the eyelets, making sure the part inside the shoes is smooth and lies flat so it won't rub against your feet.

GRACEFUL, GLAMOROUS GLOVES

BY LESLIE GELBER

Leslie says, "One of my passions is accessorizing and putting the finishing touches on that special ensemble to complete the look. Finding a box of neatly folded vintage gloves began to conjure stories from the past. Embellishing these gloves to tell those stories and add that final accent was the inspiration for my Graceful, Glamorous Gloves."

In addition to Leslie's glamorous gloves, we've included a couple of simpler pairs to get you started. You can use gloves made of soft-as-butter leather or almost any other kind of material, depending on how you want to modify them. Look for old gloves at estate sales.

Mermaid's Night Out Gloves

Materials
- cloth gloves
- scrap of cardboard
- beads
- shells
- fishing lures (optional)
- colorful sewing thread for creating machine-made lace (optional)
- water-soluble stabilizer for machine-made lace (optional) (featured, Sulky Solvy)
- ready-made lace (optional)

Tools
- scissors
- beading needle and coordinating thread
- sewing machine (optional)

Techniques
- beading

1 Cut the scrap cardboard to fit inside the gloves. This ensures that the stitches will not go through all the layers.

2 If you want to add lace, sew it in place by hand. (See the Tips box for this project for instructions on making machine-made lace.)

3 Stitch beads, shells, and lures in place all over the gloves except the palms and between the fingers—keep these areas free so that you can wear the gloves comfortably.

Purple Gloves

Materials
- leather gloves
- scrap of cardboard
- fabric paint (featured, Lumiere pearl turquoise)

Tools
- foam brush
- plastic plate or other palette
- clean rag
- foam stamp

Techniques
- painting
- stamping
- heat setting

1 Shake the paint and squirt a little onto the palette.

2 Using the foam brush and working with a small area of each glove at a time, dry brush a little paint onto the body and fingers of the glove. Immediately wipe this off with the rag, leaving only the faintest traces of paint. It is best to do a small part of each glove at a time to make sure you can wipe off most of the paint before it dries.

3 Insert the cardboard. Use the brush to apply a very thin coat of paint to the stamp, and test the stamp on the palm of the glove. If the image is gloppy, wash and dry the stamp and try again, using even less paint. (Test the palm of the other glove.) A little goes a long way, and this is more like dry brushing than like regular fabric stamping.

4 Allow the paint to dry for at least 48 hours. You can heat set the gloves, but it's not necessary unless the gloves will be laundered.

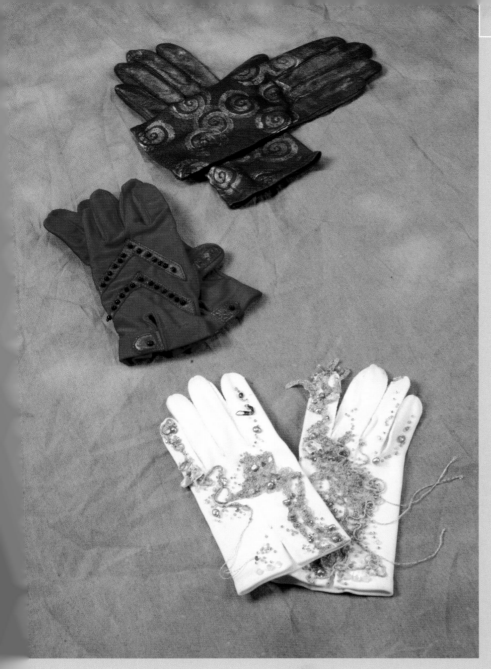

Beaded Red Gloves

Materials and Tools
- red gloves with leather trim (The sample gloves were made by Isotoner and have a perforated leather trim that was perfect for embellishing with beads)
- medium-sized black beads
- red seed beads
- beading needle and red thread

Techniques
- beading

1 Double the thread and knot it. Bring the needle from the inside up through the first perforation. If you don't have gloves with a design you want to bead, add a pattern of dots with a black pen and then bead over those.

2 Put a black bead on the needle and then add a red bead. Go back down through the black bead, through the first perforation, and then come out the second perforation. Continue across the leather trim.

3 Knot the thread on the inside and cut. Repeat for the second row of trim.

4 Add a black bead and a red bead to the cuff trim.

TIPS

To create machine-made lace, you'll do free-motion machine embroidery on a water-soluble stabilizer, such as that made by Sulky. Thread the machine and bobbin with colorful thread. Place a piece of the water-soluble stabilizer under the needle and drop the feed dogs (or cover them with the cover plate, if you have an older model machine). Begin stitching, moving the water-soluble stabilizer in a circular motion, leaving some space so that the finished piece will have an airy look. When you've made about 5" (13 cm) or so of lace, wash it according to the package directions so that the product dissolves and leaves the "lace."

✳✳✳

Couch fibers onto the cuff of the glove.

✳✳✳

Sew a tassel onto the back of each glove, making sure it won't get in the way when you wear them.

Front view

HAPPY BAG WITH MATCHING COIN PURSE

BY LYNN WHIPPLE

Materials
- purse made from an old quilt (See Tips for this project for instructions on making a purse similar to the one shown.)
- felt
- color copy of an old photograph
- black fabric ink
- muslin
- twine
- glue stick

Tools
- rubber stamps
- scissors
- pencil
- sewing machine or needle and thread

Techniques
- stamping with ink

Lynn says, "I should call this a 'permission purse' because I gave myself full permission to make it up as I went along! I'm not really much of a seamstress, but that hasn't ever stopped me!" You can find funky little hand-made purses at craft shows everywhere. Just in case they're hard to find where you live, we've included instructions for making your own bag just like this one.

1 Cut out the color copy of a photograph.

2 Cut a hat shape out of muslin to fit the head.

3 Stamp words or images on the hat and allow the ink to dry.

4 Use the glue stick to attach the photocopy and the hat to the front of the bag.

5 Cut pieces of colorful felt for accents and attach them with the glue stick.

6 Sew all pieces in place by hand or with a sewing machine.

TIPS

To make your own quilt-scrap purse, follow Lynn's steps:

1 Make a paper pattern in any shape you want. The size may depend on the size of the available quilt scraps.

2 Cut two of these shapes from the quilt scraps—one for the front and one for the back.

3 Cut one long strip and sew it to the front of the bag. For a purse like this, you'd have a strip about 3" wide by 21" long (7.5 cm x 52.5 cm). The edges will face the outside, so you'll sew the wrong sides together.

4 Sew the other side of the strip to the back of the bag.

5 For handles, cut two strips of quilt fabric about 1.5" wide by 16" long (3.5 cm x 40 cm). If you line them with felt, like the purse shown here, make the felt a little narrower, about 1" (2.5 cm) wide.

6 Sew the quilt handle to the felt.

7 Sew the handles to the inside of the front and back of the bag, going over the stitching several times for strength.

8 Cover the stitching with pieces of felt sewn on to hide the stitching.

※ ※ ※

To make the tiny change purse, use all the same materials you used for the larger bag. Decorate the front side with stamping and a piece of muslin and felt. Sew a line of stitching across the top of the front and back pieces, and then put them together and sew down the side, across the bottom, and back up, forming a little pouch shape. Add twine for a handle, sewing back and forth over it for strength and covering the stitching with tiny pieces of felt.

※ ※ ※

The back of this bag has a muslin flower with a red felt center that was sewn with red thread just like the photocopy and hat on the front.

※ ※ ※

The paper photocopy and the felt prevent this bag from being washable. Luckily the aged fabric of the quilt will make minor stains unnoticeable. To create a similar effect on a garment that has to be washed, make an iron-on transfer of the photograph and use flannel instead of felt.

SUMMERTIME DRESS

BY RICË FREEMAN-ZACHERY

Materials

- cotton dress
- white cotton fabric
- scraps of fabric in colors to coordinate with the dress (a bandanna from the craft store was used in the sample)
- iron-on transfers (you can take your photos to a copy shop to have this done or make them yourself with your computer, scanner, inkjet printer, and transfer paper)
- fabric paint
- fusible webbing
- fibers
- beads

Tools

- scissors
- pins
- button covering kit
- rubber stamps
- foam brush for applying fabric paint to stamps
- iron and ironing board
- embroidery needle and thread
- beading needle
- sewing machine or needle and thread

Techniques

- stamping with fabric paint
- image transfers
- appliqué
- couching
- beading
- buttons
- heat setting

Yellow is not my favorite color, but this sunny dress just begged to be made into a tribute to my favorite time of the year. It's embellished with favorite summertime emblems: transfers of El Sol, from a deck of Loteria cards, and some fuzzy yellow fiber that had been waiting for a home. It's a lot of fun to find things that work together, like the colors in El Sol and the fabric paint, the yellow fiber and the summery bandanna used to cover the buttons. When I found the yellow-orange beads, I knew I was set.

1. Stamp the text and images. The sample has black fabric paint for the words and orange paint for the sun. Let the paint dry for 48 hours, then heat set it before adding any three-dimensional embellishments, such as fibers, transfers, or beads.

2. While you're waiting for the paint to cure, make the transfers and iron them onto muslin or cotton in a pale color that coordinates with your garment. Remember that the transfers are transparent and colored fabric will change the color of the image.

3. Cut the muslin a little larger than the transferred image and fray the edges, if desired. If not, turn under the edges and press them in place, preparing your appliqués for sewing.

4. Choose the size of the button covering kit you want to use. If the garment will slip over your head, as this dress does, you can use any size buttons and sew them in place over the buttonholes, since they don't have to be functional. Cover the buttons according to the package instructions using a coordinating fabric—check tie-dyed bandannas at the craft store or fat quarters at a quilt shop for some really cool prints.

5. When the paint has cured, heat set it.

6. Appliqué the transfers.

7. Couch the fiber with a coordinating thread, either with a zigzag stitch on a sewing machine or by hand. The yellow fiber in the sample was couched with orange thread.

8. Add beads. The sample has beading on the stamped suns on the bodice only. It would look great to bead all of them, depending on how much time you can spend on the dress.

Plain cotton garments are great for altering. If they're not the color you want, dye them first.

✻ ✻ ✻

In choosing a dress, think about how much time you want to spend on the project. A larger, fuller dress will have more space to embellish, while a more tapered garment will look richer and more lavish with less work.

SALVAGED DENIM JACKET

BY RICË FREEMAN-ZACHERY

Materials

- denim jacket
- iron-on transfers (you can take your photos to a copy shop to have this done or make them yourself with your computer, scanner, inkjet printer, and transfer paper)
- fabric paint
- scrap of fabric
- fusible webbing
- beads

Tools

- scissors
- pins
- stamps
- small paintbrush
- foam brush
- iron and ironing board
- embroidery needle and thread
- beading needle
- sewing machine or needle and thread

Techniques

- ripping and tearing
- mending
- stamping with fabric paint
- image transfers
- painting fabric
- appliqué
- embroidery
- beading
- heat setting

My husband found this abandoned jacket years ago. It was wonderfully soft and faded, and after I laundered it, I started embroidering the seams that had begun to wear. I wore it for years, working on it whenever it needed repair. Then, when I began working with iron-on transfers, I decided to put one of my husband on the back, using his second-grade school photograph. I found a photo of a little boy in a cowboy outfit and inserted my husband's face and transferred the resulting picture onto fabric my husband picked out. I stamped the words, added the beads, and wore the jacket to the school where I was substituting and where my husband teaches and coaches. The kids loved it. I later added the transfers of the phrenology head and my own face. I'm not finished yet; I'll keep working on the jacket until there's not an empty space left.

1   Use a sturdy embroidery stitch, such as the split stitch (page 45), to reinforce all the seams that are worn. You can use a rainbow of colors for this, or you can choose just one or two colors.

2   Adhere an iron-on transfer on muslin or colored cotton fabric, as I did on the back of the sample jacket. Turn under the edges and prepare as an appliqué. Set it aside. Pin the paper backing from the transfer to the jacket where you want the appliqué to go. This serves as a guide when you stamp the letters; you'll sew the appliqué on near the end of the project, just before adding the beads.

3   Stamp all the words with fabric paint, allow the paint to cure for 48 hours, then heat set before embroidering.

4   Embroider the letters, if desired. Edging with a split stitch, as shown in the sample, makes them look as if they were appliquéd, rather than just stamped.

5   Use opaque paint to highlight some of the features on the two faces. To heat set this paint, cover the transfer with waxed paper before ironing (so the transfer won't stick to the iron).

6   Use fabric glue to hold the appliqués in place, or attach them with fusible webbing, following the package directions. Sew around the edges to ensure permanence. Embroidery thread and a split stitch secure the appliqué and add a nice dimensional look to the finished piece, but you can use regular thread and invisible stitching. Blanket stitching on a machine works well, too.

7   Add the beads last, highlighting any areas that need a little sparkle.

You can add paint directly to the jacket, or you can bleach parts of it with a bleaching pen.

❋ ❋ ❋

If the jacket has holes, patch them with colorful fabric. Scraps of velvet or velveteen work well for patching. (See Patching Holes, page 18.)

❋ ❋ ❋

You can periodically do more stitching on the seams as they show signs of wear. Think of your jacket as a work in progress, adding to it whenever it needs repair or you get a new idea. It can serve as a sampler for trying new techniques. If you don't like the results, you can always remove them, cover them up, or turn them into something else.

ANIMAL FAIR DENIM DRESS

BY JENNIFER CRUTCHER

Materials

- denim dress
- white muslin
- scraps of fabric with animal images
- scrap of black fleece
- iron-on transfers of "Animal Fair" lines printed from a computer
- anti-fray adhesive (featured, Fray Block)
- multicolored all-purpose thread
- buttons in various colors and sizes
- fabric adhesive

Tools

- scissors
- iron and ironing board
- sewing machine or needle and thread
- embroidery needle and multicolored thread

Techniques

- image transfers
- appliqué
- embroidery
- buttons

TIPS

For about $25, you can buy a small sewing machine that will create a simple running stitch.

Add beads or tiny bells to the stuffed animals.

Jennifer wanted to make a dress that was not only fun for her daughter, Mikaela, to wear, but that was easy to make and relied on words, rather than images, to decorate the garment. She needed the dress in time for a party, and this technique was the perfect solution.

1. Prepare iron-on transfers of words. Cut these apart and iron them on white muslin. Leave a large border around each word.
2. Use a dot of fabric adhesive to hold the words in place while you sew. Stitch around the edges with the multicolored thread and a running stitch. You can do this by hand or machine.
3. Sew buttons along the bottom edge.
4. Using the multicolored embroidery thread, stitch random small stitches among the word blocks.
5. Make faux stuffed animals for the pockets: Lay the animal print fabric face up on the black fleece and stitch around various animal shapes. Run a small bead of the anti-fray adhesive along the stitch lines and allow it to dry. Cut out each animal close to the lines of stitching. Add decorative stitching to each animal as desired. Place the animals in the pockets.

TIKI ART JEANS

BY ALLENE SHACKELFORD

Allene has always loved everything tiki—from the music to kitschy 1950s South Sea art to a well-made Mai Tai—so these jeans were a natural for her. She recommends listening to the two-CD set *The Exotic Sounds of Martin Denny* as you make your Tiki Art Jeans.

Materials

- jeans
- 1 yard (1 m) of white rayon lining fabric
- four packages of white iron-on patch material
- one package of light blue iron-on hem tape, 1/2" (1 cm) wide
- blue thread
- permanent pigment ink (featured, Crafter's Ink, brown, ochre, moss green, dune, cranberry red, coral, and black)
- permanent dye ink (featured, Ancient Page, coal black, sienna, and pine)
- shrink plastic, such as Lucky Squirrel Brand artist's grade shrink plastic, canvas white
- assorted bamboo and glass beads
- small shells
- waxed paper
- copy paper
- permanent adhesive, such as E600 glue

Tools

- rubber stamps
- chalk stick
- straight pins
- 320 grit sandpaper
- paper towels
- heat gun or toaster oven
- assorted metal tiki charms
- scissors
- iron and ironing board
- sewing machine or needle and thread

Techniques

- ripping and tearing
- mending
- patching holes
- beading

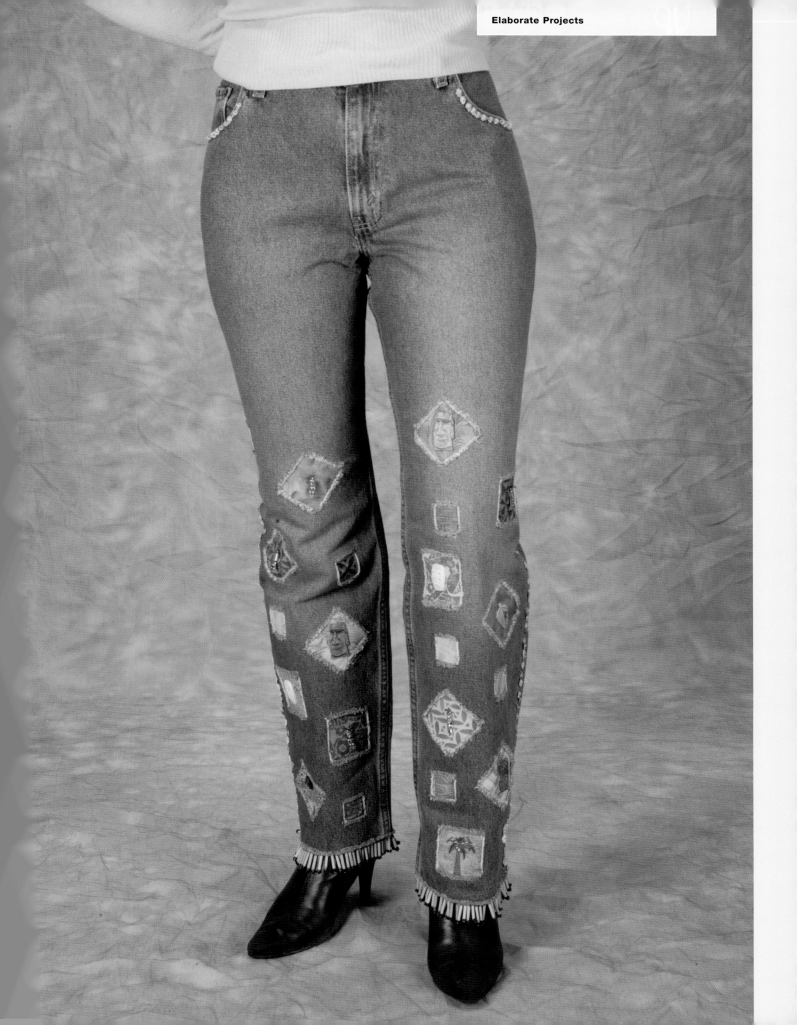

PREPARING JEANS

1   Draw a 2" x 2" (5 cm x 5 cm) square pattern on copy paper and cut it out. Repeat with a 1" x 1" (2.5 cm x 2.5 cm) square. Make six or seven of each.

2   Lay out jeans and place patterns on the legs in a random manner. Mark each square on the denim with a sharpened chalk stick.

3   Cut out the squares with sharp scissors. Take care to cut only on the chalked lines. This will leave little cutout squares on the pant legs. Trim off the hem of the jeans as well.

4   Wash and dry the jeans without fabric softener. When the jeans are dry, you will see holes framed by frayed denim. Resist the urge to trim loose threads.

5   Next open the outer seams on each leg with a seam ripper, all the way up to the highest square hole in each leg. This will make the machine stitching on the holes much easier.

CREATING FABRIC INSERTS

1   Cut the rayon lining fabric into rough 4" x 4" (10 cm x 10 cm) squares, one for each hole.

2   Lay these squares on copy paper to protect your work surface. Apply the pigment ink directly to the rayon squares. Layer colors or sponge on additional colors. Allow the ink to dry overnight and then heat set, first with the heat tool for two minutes to completely dry the ink. Finish heat setting with an iron.

3   Stamp cooled squares with selected background designs using permanent dye ink. Let the ink dry and heat set it with an iron.

4   Use the 2" x 2" (5 cm x 5 cm) pattern and chalk to mark squares on the decorated rayon pieces. Repeat with the 1" x 1" (2.5 cm x 2.5 cm) squares. Measure and mark $1/4$" (0.5 cm) out from the chalk lines to form a larger square.

5   Cut on the outer lines with scissors.

6   Lay the rayon piece on top of the iron-on patch material (adhesive side up), mark and cut an additional $1/4$" (0.5 cm) and trim. You will have a layered insert unit with the rayon on top and the $1/4$" (0.5 cm) larger iron-on patch on the bottom.

7   Next place the insert unit on an ironing board. Make sure the rayon is face up on the adhesive side of the patch material. Cover with waxed paper and iron on medium heat for only 10 seconds to attach the rayon to the patch. Allow it to cool for 10 seconds, then gently pull the patch unit from the waxed paper.

ASSEMBLING RAYON/PATCH INSERTS

1   Arrange patch units under each hole with colors alternating. Pin in place or take a digital photo to evaluate and aid in placement.

2   Starting with the bottom hole in each leg, lay the patch unit under the hole and center, matching chalk lines. Remove any pins.

3   Press near frayed edges on the outside of the hole with a medium heat dry iron. Do not press on the rayon center. This will adhere the outer $1/4$" (0.5 cm) of iron-on patch material to the edges of the hole in the jeans.

4   When the patch is lightly tacked in place, flip the leg over and iron over the whole patch for 5 seconds. Then iron around each edge of the patch for 10 seconds to adhere the entire unit to the leg material. Repeat with the remaining squares.

5   Use a sewing machine and blue thread to sew tightly around all the holes to prevent further fraying of the edges. Trim off any long threads.

CREATING THE HEM FRINGE

1   Pin hemming tape onto the leg hem area, adding a few inches (centimeters) to each end. Cut the tape.

2   Remove the pins. Start 1" (2.5 cm) in and sew bamboo beads in a row along the bottom of the tape, using smaller beads as anchors. Knot every few inches to hold beads securely.

3 Pin finished fringe, with iron-on adhesive facing the denim, onto the bottom of each leg under the frayed edge.

4 Iron the fringe in place, removing the pins as you go.

5 To make the fringe secure, machine stitch the hem tape in place, sewing on the right side above the frayed hem on each leg.

MAKING SHRINK PLASTIC ELEMENTS

1 Sand the shrink plastic sheet and wipe off the residue. Lightly apply pigment ink directly from the pad to the sanded plastic for background color.

2 Ink the stamp with black pigment ink. Stamp on copy paper and then stamp on the plastic.

3 Cut out the image, being careful not to smudge the ink. The image will look very light, but it will darken upon shrinking.

4 Punch a $1/8$" (3 mm) hole in charm if desired.

5 Follow the manufacturer's instructions for shrinking, heating either with a heat gun or in a toaster oven. The times will vary according to the brand of plastic you choose. (See Tips for this project.)

FINAL ASSEMBLY

1 Decide on the placement of the decorative elements.

2 Turn the jeans inside out and pin the outer seams. Machine stitch on the seam lines. Stitch again or zigzag to prevent fraying.

3 Turn the jeans right side out and sew on the charms. Glue or sew shrink plastic elements to the jeans. Glue the shells on the pockets. Allow the glue to dry thoroughly before wearing the jeans.

TIPS

Hand wash the jeans in cool water with a gentle cleaner, such as Woolite. Hand rinse with fabric softener and hang to dry.

✄ ✄ ✄

An easier way to create a similar fringed hem would be to purchase a beaded fringe and simply stitch it in place.

✄ ✄ ✄

If you want to be able to machine wash and dry your jeans, you'll need to stitch things in place, rather than using glue. You'll also need to test everything for permanence first.

✄ ✄ ✄

Lucky Squirrel shrink plastic is highly recommended by the artist. Their website provides excellent instructions for its use. (See Resources, page 121.)

ASIAN FLAIR PURSE

BY ANNE SAGOR

Materials

- denim purse with plain front flap
- paper to use as a pattern
- various Asian-themed print fabrics
- iron-on transfer of an image (The artist used part of a poster for the image of the two women.)
- acrylic paints (featured, Accent Crown Jewels, Tiara Ruby, and DecoArt Dazzling Metallics, Emperor's Gold)
- small iron-on appliqué of a dragon (This was purchased, but you can create your own.)
- buttons (The artist used handmade polymer clay buttons.)
- replica of a Chinese coin
- vintage (or newly created) beaded appliqué
- decorative ribbon
- fusible webbing (featured, Stitch Witchery)
- permanent fabric glue (featured, Jones Tones Plexi 400 Stretch Adhesive)
- anti-fray adhesive (featured, Fray Check)

Tools

- scissors
- rubber stamps
- cosmetic sponge wedges
- Styrofoam tray or acrylic palette
- hair dryer (optional, to speed the drying of acrylic paints)
- iron and ironing board
- sewing machine and thread

Techniques

- stamping with acrylic paint
- image transfers
- appliqué

Anne found this purse when she was sorting through her mother's things. Her mother had embroidered her own initials on an insert on the flap of the purse, which Anne removed and plans to make into a pillow. For the bag itself, she was inspired by a large bead-and-sequin appliqué of a Chinese dragon. Even though the dragon itself wasn't used on the purse, it provided the theme.

1. Squeeze the acrylic paint onto the tray or palette and apply it to the stamps with the cosmetic sponges.

2. Stamp the various images on all exposed parts of the purse except the front and back of the purse flap.

3. Make a paper pattern of the front of the purse flap. Use this to cut a piece of textured or Asian-print fabric for the background of the collage.

4. Create your transfer. Here the image was printed directly on prepared fabric.

5. Cut a section of Asian calligraphy from commercial fabric. Arrange this section, the transfer, the small dragon appliqué, and any other elements for the collage. When you have a pleasing arrangement, use a fabric glue stick to hold the pieces in place.

6. Using a zigzag or other decorative stitch, sew all elements into place.

7. Sew the collage to the front of the purse flap. You can turn under the edges or leave them flat and cover them with the stitching.

8. Sew a strip of decorative ribbon across the top of the flap and secure the ends on the reverse side. Use anti-fray adhesive on the ends if necessary to prevent unraveling, or just turn the edges under before stitching in place.

9. Use the paper pattern to cut a piece of fabric to line the inside of the flap.

10. Apply anti-fray adhesive to the edges and allow it to dry.

11. Sandwich fusible webbing between the fabric and the inside of the flap and iron to fuse. Stitch around the edges for security, if desired, making sure the stitching doesn't show on the front of the flap.

12. Cut the beaded vintage appliqué into pieces as needed and apply anti-fray adhesive to all exposed edges. Allow it to dry. Attach to the collaged purse flap with permanent fabric glue. Put waxed paper over it and weigh it down with a book. Let it dry overnight.

13. Attach the other decorative elements with glue. Weigh those down and allow the glue to dry overnight.

PATCHWORK BAG

BY RICË FREEMAN-ZACHERY

Materials

- canvas or fabric bag
- scraps of fabric
- paper for creating a pattern
- fibers and trims
- beads
- fusible webbing or fabric glue stick

Tools

- scissors
- pencil or pen
- pins
- sewing machine or needle and thread
- iron and ironing board
- embroidery needle and thread
- beading needle

Techniques

- beading
- couching
- embroidery
- crazy quilting

TIPS

You can cover the edges with decorative braid or trim to hide the seams.

✖✖✖

Instead of covering the entire bag, cover just parts of it, adding patches of fabric to the front and back. Make transfers of photographs or other images, iron those on muslin, and sew them on as patches.

✖✖✖

Add fringe to the bag. You can attach purchased fringe or create your own beaded fringe. (See Beaded Fringe, page 52.)

This is a great disguise for a fabric or canvas bag that's sturdy and serviceable but not very attractive. Use the bag for a base and cover it with stamped and painted muslin or other solid fabric or a patchwork, as shown in the sample. I had a lot of scraps of material that I really liked—a piece of ruby velvet from a dress my mother made for me when I was two, some soft scraps of my husband's worn-out silk pajamas, bits and pieces of fabric that were too small to use by themselves but too interesting to throw away. Sewn together, with the addition of beading, embroidery, and couching, they form a rich patchwork. Add buttons, pins, or other decorative embellishments as a final touch.

1   Lay the bag flat and trace around it to make a rough pattern for the cover. You'll want the pattern to be a little larger than the bag itself. Since you're going to fold the fabric to the inside and sew it in place, it doesn't have to be exact—you can adjust the fit as you sew.

2   Lay out your fabric scraps and pin the edges together, using the paper pattern as a guide.

3   When you're pleased with the arrangement, sew them together, pressing open the seams with an iron as you go. You can do this on the sewing machine or by hand, as you would a crazy quilt. (See Easy Crazy Quilting, page 19.) You should have two large pieces of patchwork: one for the front and one for the back of the bag. Set these aside.

4   Cover the handle with a long strip of fabric. Use fabric glue or fusible webbing to hold this in place as you wrap it around the existing handle, fold under the edges, and tack one overlapping the other. On this bag, the handle fabric goes all the way around the bottom of the bag, and the part where it joins the two sides is covered with a couched trim.

5   Embellish the front and back pieces with embroidery, beading, and couching.

6   Place the front and back panels over the bag and tack them into place with stitching, fabric glue, or pins. You can fold the top edges of the cover to the inside of the bag or turn them under right at the edge, whip stitching the edge of the cover to the edge of the bag.

7   Continue attaching the panels all the way around.

8   After you've sewn everything securely in place, embellish with any larger beads, buttons, or trim you've selected.

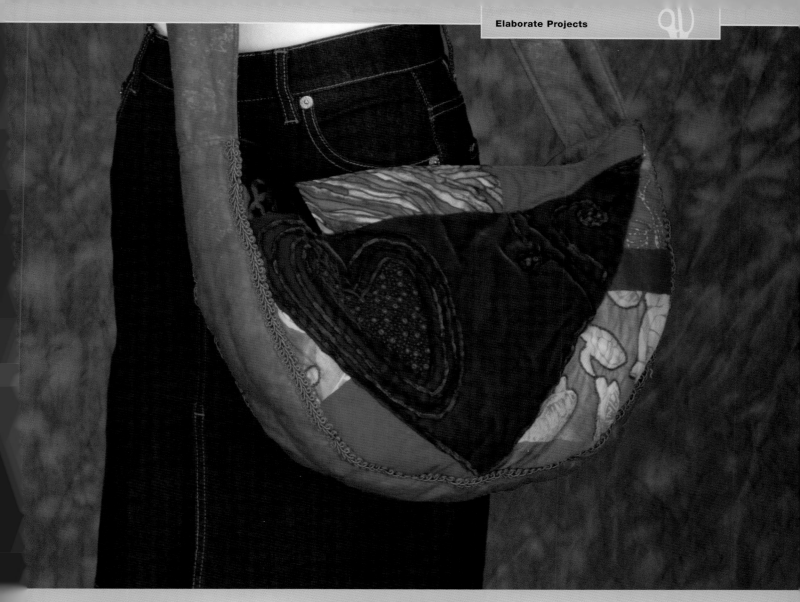

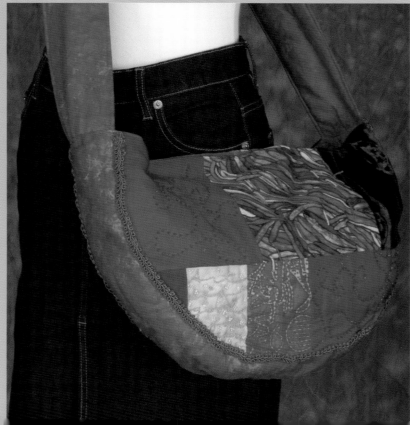

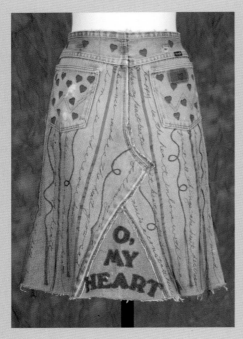

TIPS

For a rainbow skirt, use many different colors of thread and fibers—it's a great way to use up bits and pieces left over from other projects.

✳ ✳ ✳

Some fibers are going to shrink, and some will knot up in the laundry. Either test them first by stitching a length on a piece of scrap muslin and laundering it, or be prepared to replace the ones that cause problems. (I don't test mine, and I've never had trouble except for some slight knotting in the fuzzier fibers.)

✳ ✳ ✳

For added sturdiness, I stitched a piece of fabric on the inside of the skirt, over the threads holding the beads and sequins in place, just to make sure those threads don't get pulled or broken.

O, MY HEART JOURNAL SKIRT

BY RICË FREEMAN-ZACHERY

Materials

- denim skirt
- fabric paint
- scrap of fabric for patching holes
- ribbon
- red heart buttons
- sequins
- beads
- fabric glue stick

Tools

- scissors
- pins
- stamps
- foam brush for applying fabric paint to your stamps
- permanent ink pen, such as Lumocolor or Adirondack pens
- sewing machine or needle and thread
- iron and ironing board or commercial clothes dryer
- embroidery needle and thread
- beading needle

Techniques

- ripping and tearing
- mending
- adding words and letters
- couching
- embroidery
- using sequins
- heat setting
- transforming jeans into a skirt

This romantic skirt began as an experiment with sequins. I saw a handmade book with a sequined heart on every page; I loved the way the hearts sparkled and wondered if it would work on a skirt. I drew a heart outline and began adding beads and sequins. Sewing on each individual sequin and bead by hand is time-consuming, but it makes quite a statement. The sequins hold up fine—just hand wash or use a gentle cycle when cleaning.

1 Make the skirt from a pair of jeans, patching any holes.

2 Couch the ribbon, tucking under the top end and stopping the stitching a couple of inches from the bottom edge, so that the ends will move when you wear it.

3 Draw lines between the couched ribbons and embroider those lines with the embroidery thread.

4 Stamp the hearts and the title with fabric paint. Use the pen to write quotes in all the spaces between the thread and ribbons. Let the paint and ink cure at least 48 hours before heat setting. If your ribbons and embroidery thread are heat-sensitive, protect them with a pressing cloth and heat set from the back of the skirt or put the skirt in a commercial dryer for 30 minutes.

5 Embroider around the stamped letters.

6 Draw a heart on the front panel of the skirt and sew on the beads and sequins. If you can't bear to sew it by hand, buy a sequined patch or use one cut from another garment.

7 Sew the heart buttons to the top of the couched ribbons to hold them down. Trim the bottoms of the ribbons at an angle to prevent excessive fraying.

LOVER'S EYES: REMEMBRANCE VEST

BY ROZ STENDAHL

Materials

- black vest (The artist used a 100% linen vest from Flax.)
- 1 yard (1 m) finely woven, bright white cotton fabric
- transparent fabric paints (featured, Setacolor Transparent Fabric Paints)
- fabric screen images made from Print Gocco and a photocopy

Tools

- Print Gocco—both the Print Gocco B6 unit and the Fabric Printing unit
- photocopier that uses toner
- washing machine and dryer
- scissors
- pins
- aluminum foil
- spray bottle of water
- paintbrush
- iron and ironing board
- sewing machine or needle and thread
- thread to coordinate with colored fabric
- variegated thread
- buttons

Techniques

- painting fabric
- using Print Gocco

"Lover's eyes" were small paintings of the eye of a loved one, popular in the late eighteenth and early nineteenth centuries. They were painted without the face so the lover's identity would remain a secret. Later, the eyes of family members, especially those being mourned, were worn in brooches or bracelets. Here, Roslyn uses a drawing of the eyes of her beloved dog, Dottie, to create a remembrance vest.

Roslyn explains, "The fabric appliqué has frayed edges to symbolize how her death tore the fabric of my life. Many cultures tear their clothing or wear patches to commemorate the death of a loved one. The stitching that connects the images is symbolic of the way in which Dottie connected everything in life for me and protected me. When worn, the images on the vest start at the heart and work around the entire body."

1 Make a copy of your image on a standard photocopy machine.

2 Make a fabric screen of the image following the Print Gocco instructions on page 32.

3 Wash and dry the white cotton without fabric softener.

4 Mix fabric paints in the colors you want, keeping in mind that the fabric should be light enough that the Print Gocco images will show up well.

5 Paint the fabric.

6 Scrunch up the fabric so that the paint will dry in a mottled pattern. (See Tips on Painting Fabric, page 24.) Allow the paint to dry for 48 hours.

7 Heat set the paint by ironing it for five minutes.

8 Print your Print Gocco image on several pieces of the painted fabric. Make a couple extra prints of each image for backup.

9 Allow the fabric to dry overnight and then heat set for two minutes.

10 Cut out the images, leaving as large a border as you want. Fray the edges of the squares and baste in place on the vest.

11 Sew in place using colored thread and decorative stitching. Each piece has several lines of zigzag sewing in different colors of thread.

12 Use variegated thread to sew a wavy line of stitching to connect all the patches around the vest.

13 Replace the buttons.

TIPS

Roz is an illustrator by profession and draws from life. Here she used parts of the hundreds of sketches she drew of Dottie during their years together. If you don't feel comfortable drawing, though, there are easy ways to achieve a hand-sketched look. Use a photograph to draw or trace the eyes—or entire face—to be copied. Or take a photo of your pet and enlarge just the face and make a photocopy of that. If you have software that lets you adjust images on your computer, you can scan in the photograph, adjust it, print it out on your printer, and take that inkjet image to the copy shop for a toner copy for your Print Gocco.

✳ ✳ ✳

The garment doesn't have to be a memorial. You could make a celebratory garment with images of your whole family—both two-legged and four-legged members.

✳ ✳ ✳

If even tracing a photograph seems intimidating, start off with one of the thousands of copyright-free clip art images from Dover. (See Resources, page 121.)

You can add as much stitching and beading as you'd like to make your vest really sparkle.

❋ ❋ ❋

Add covered buttons to replace existing buttons or as a purely decorative embellishment.

❋ ❋ ❋

If you can't find a vest, you can make one so easily that you won't believe you're sewing. Either buy a simple pattern or create one yourself by lying on a piece of paper and having someone trace around your upper body. The vest's simple shape and construction lends itself perfectly to experimentation.

❋ ❋ ❋

Lengthen a vest pattern to make a tunic.

COWGIRL SHRINE VEST

BY RICË FREEMAN-ZACHERY

Materials

- muslin vest
- iron-on transfers
- personal computer
- fabric paint
- 1 to 2 yards (1 m to 2 m) of muslin, depending on the size of the vest (This will be used as a lining and iron-on transfers.)
- fabric glue stick or fusible webbing
- beads
- paper

Tools

- seam ripper
- scissors
- pins
- stamps
- foam brush for applying fabric paint to your stamps
- black and red markers
- iron and ironing board
- sewing machine or needle and thread
- embroidery needle and thread
- beading needle

Techniques

- ripping and tearing
- mending
- adding words and letters
- image transfers
- embroidery
- beading

In the spring of 2003, the National Cowgirl Hall of Fame and Museum opened in Fort Worth, Texas. It's a beautiful building, and the exhibits are both informative and a lot of fun—you can take a grainy, old-fashioned-looking black-and-white video of yourself riding a bucking bronco (well, the top half of a mechanical horse). The video will be on the museum's website for long enough that you can go home and see it on your computer. The gift shop is full of all kinds of cowgirl-related paraphernalia that sent my imagination skyward.

For this vest, I used images scanned from books and postcards. If you're making something just for yourself, you don't have to worry about copyright laws. It's much better to create your own images if you plan to design items to sell—if you can draw, a vest like this would be even more distinctive! If not, look for clipart images of cowgirls, or go through family photos for some of those kid-on-a-pony pictures that were so popular in the 1950s and 1960s.

1 Rip out the seams on the vest and iron the pieces flat. Pin each piece to muslin and cut a duplicate piece—this will be the lining, which will both hide the embroidery stitching and provide fullness for the ragged edges. Lay the lining aside.

2 Create all the transfers and iron them onto smaller pieces of muslin. Arrange them on the vest to determine where they'll go and use pins or paper patterns to mark their placement. Set them aside.

3 Create the shrine using the instructions for Making a Shrine Appliqué on page 42.

4 Stamp all the text, using permanent fabric paint. Let the paint cure for 48 hours before heat setting with an iron.

5 Embroider the letters and add beads as desired.

6 Use a fabric glue stick to hold the transfers in place while you stitch them by hand or with a sewing machine.

7 Attach the shrine to the back of the vest, stitching about 1" (2.5 cm) in from the edges.

8 Reassemble the vest, matching up each piece with its lining. (I sewed this by hand, but a machine is also fine. I sewed the lining to the vest and then sewed the seams, all with a split stitch and blue embroidery thread. Then I went back over every visible stitch to create a solid line. This took time, but I liked the effect.)

9 Clip all the edges as described in Ripping and Tearing on page 14. Cut almost up to the stitched line; the cuts should be about $1/2$" (1 cm) apart. When you've made all the cuts, take the vest outdoors and shake it vigorously. Loose threads will fly everywhere, and that means they won't be coming loose in your washing machine.

10 Wash and dry the vest to create the ragged edges. Iron the vest if necessary, remembering to put a pressing cloth or waxed paper over the transfers before ironing.

STORY DRESS

BY RICË FREEMAN-ZACHERY

Materials

- soft chambray dress
- iron-on transfers (you can take your photos to a copy shop to have this done or make them yourself with your computer, scanner, inkjet printer, and transfer paper)
- fabric paint
- scrap of fabric (featured, pink cotton gauze)
- crystal organdy
- fusible webbing or fabric glue stick
- beads

Tools

- scissors
- seam ripper
- pins
- heavy cardboard, mat board, or cutting mat
- stamps
- foam brush
- iron and ironing board
- sewing machine or needle and thread
- embroidery needle and thread
- beading needle

Techniques

- ripping and tearing
- stamping with fabric paint
- embroidery
- image transfers
- beading
- heat setting

This was another inexpensive thrift shop find. It had a high rounded neck and little cap sleeves, which I didn't care for, but the fabric was wonderful, so I bought it. I cut off the sleeves and the neck and then, figuring I'd already taken the plunge, cut off the hem, too. I sewed a line of embroidery around those edges to secure them, and then I stamped a story and added some transfers of myself at age two. Some more embroidery, some beads, and some wisps of organdy—also with transferred photos—completed my *Story Dress*.

1. Adjust the basic shape of the dress as desired using scissors and a seam ripper. For example, shorten a hem, remove sleeves, or adjust a neckline.

2. If you cut off sleeves and hems, secure the edges so they won't fray. Some fabrics won't fray much; and if you know yours is one of them, you can leave the edges completely raw. Otherwise, sew or embroider around all the cut or torn edges.

3. Do all the stamping and painting first, using the cutting mat or mat board under the fabric for stability. Let the paint cure for 48 hours before heat setting.

4. While you're waiting for the paint to cure, work on the transfers. If desired, add color to the transfers before ironing them to fabric. (See Tips for Transfers, page 36.) On the sample, some are ironed onto 100% nylon crystal organdy and some onto cotton gauze— these two completely different fabrics have different requirements for transferring. (See Transferring to Sheer Fabrics, page 38.)

5. After heat setting the paint, do all the embroidery and beading around the letters before appliquéing the transfers.

6. Appliqué the transfers, using a fabric glue stick to hold them in place while you sew or embroider around the edges.

7. Add more stitching and beading as desired.

8. Finally, attach the floating strips of organdy to the shoulders, tacking them in place with beads or buttons.

TIPS

The strips of organdy were cut before ironing on the transfers— they will keep fraying and shedding and will probably eventually have to be removed, but I'm pleased with the way they look, even after laundering. Remember that nothing has to be permanent, and you can keep altering indefinitely.

⚜ ⚜ ⚜

If you want to add something that can't be laundered, think of various methods of temporary attachment: buttons and button-holes, snaps, ribbon ties. For the organdy overlay, I could have made buttonholes to fit over buttons sewn to the dress. The same technique would have worked for the floating strips of fabric on the shoulders, or I could have sewn a piece of ribbon to each shoulder and used those to tie onto the fabric.

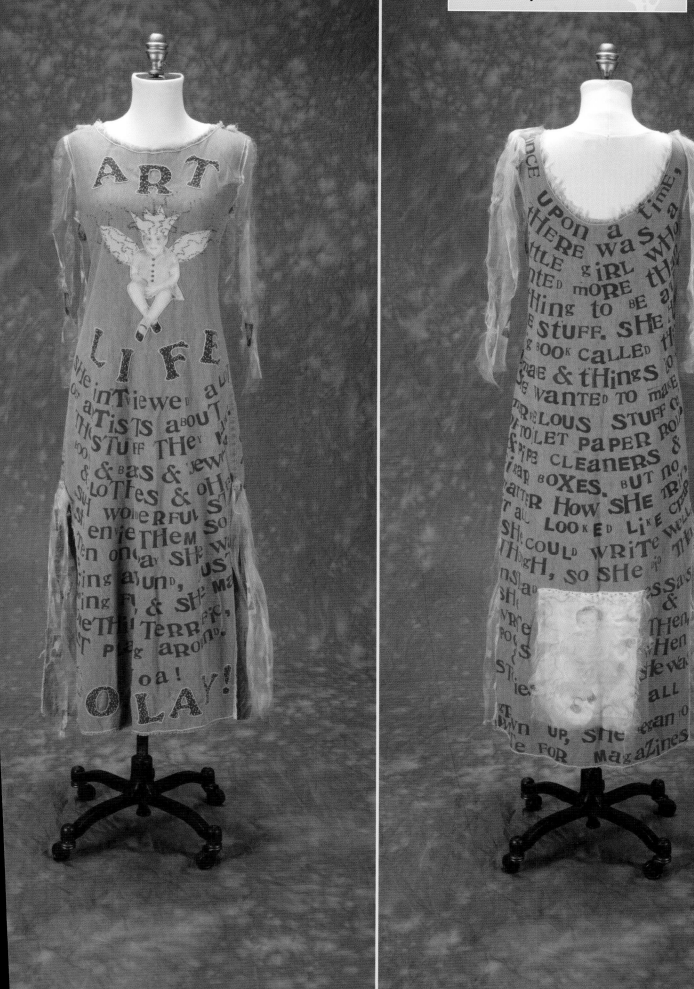

HAIRCUT JOURNAL SKIRT

BY RICË FREEMAN-ZACHERY

Materials

- denim skirt
- iron-on transfers (you can take your photos to a copy shop to have this done or make them yourself with your computer, scanner, inkjet printer, and transfer paper)
- fabric paint
- scrap of fabric
- fusible webbing or fabric glue stick

Tools

- scissors
- pins
- stamps
- foam brush
- iron and ironing board
- sewing machine or needle and thread
- embroidery needle and thread

Techniques

- ripping and tearing
- mending
- transforming jeans into a skirt
- stamping with fabric paint
- image transfers
- painting fabric
- appliqué
- embroidery
- beading

When I turned 42, I cut off the hip-length hair I'd had almost all my life. A fellow artist went with me to the salon and documented the momentous event in pictures. I used them to create this journal skirt. The techniques aren't difficult, but this isn't a quick project: I worked on it for over a year, adding more photos as my hair got shorter and shorter—and redder and redder. Journal skirts are perfect for recording big adventures.

1   Make any adjustments to the skirt, or create a skirt from a pair of jeans. (See Transforming Jeans into a Skirt, page 15.) Here, heavy muslin is used for the panels in the front and back. Cut off the waist band and remove the loops, then patch those and any other holes with scraps of coordinating fabric.

2   Make your iron-on transfers. Iron some of them on muslin and save some to iron directly on the panels of the skirt. Arrange them on the skirt to figure out where you want them to go, then mark that with pins or paper patterns temporarily attached. Set the transfers aside.

3   Stamp the images and stamp or write all the text. In the sample, a hand-carved stamp of a pair of scissors is used to stamp randomly on the skirt, filling up some of the blank spaces. They are also stamped next to the patched holes in the back of the skirt. Let the paint cure for 48 hours, and then heat set it.

4   Embroider around the letters. Add other embroidery, such as lines and squiggles.

5   Use fusible webbing or a fabric glue stick to hold the muslin appliqués while you sew them in place.

6   Stitch the appliqués in place, using whatever kind of stitch you like. You can use invisible stitching, a blanket stitch, or a very visible random stitch similar to the one used in the sample.

ALTERED PEOPLE COAT

BY KEELY BARHAM

Materials

- coat
- iron-on transfers (you can take your photos to a copy shop to have this done or make them yourself with your computer, scanner, inkjet printer, and transfer paper)
- white cotton fabric
- black velveteen fabric
- denim fabric
- large sheets of white paper
- freezer paper
- matching thread
- multicolored thread
- iron-on adhesive (featured, Wonder Under)

Tools

- button covering kit
- seam ripper
- pencil
- scissors
- pins
- iron and ironing board
- sewing machine

Techniques

- image transfers
- embroidery
- buttons

Keely says, "This coat, bought at a discount store, has hung in my closet for about a year without being worn. The price was right, but it was just a little too weird. As an altered coat, I think it has more potential. The people transfers were inspired by dolls that I have made in the past using the same images."

1   Use the seam ripper to rip out all of the hems, the side seams, and the underarm seams so you can work on each panel separately.

2   Trace each panel (back panel, two front panels, and two panels for each sleeve) of the coat onto the white paper to make patterns. Cut a wavy shape for the top of each panel and a straight edge for the bottoms. These are the patterns for the denim fabric.

3   Use these patterns to cut slightly shorter patterns for the black velveteen.

4   Using the patterns, cut the denim and velveteen fabric panels for each section.

5   Lay the denim panels on each section of the coat. Lay the velveteen over the denim and then pin in place, adjusting as necessary.

6   On the sewing machine, baste the layers to each panel of the coat.

7   Switch the machine to a satin stitch and sew along all the wavy edges of both fabrics, using thread that matches each.

8   Create the iron-on transfers.

9   Once the doll images have been transferred to white fabric, iron adhesive on the back and cut them out. If you use standard iron-on transfers, remember to cover them with waxed paper before ironing the adhesive to the back.

10 Lay the images on the velveteen and lightly iron in place.

11 On the sewing machine, appliqué each piece with variegated thread. The artist used a machine blanket stitch. If your machine doesn't have a blanket stitch, use a narrow zigzag stitch.

12 After all the people are appliquéd, use the same variegated thread to do free-motion machine embroidery in all the blank spaces of the velveteen.

13 Re-stitch all the coat seams and hems.

14 Replace the buttons with velveteen buttons the same size, made from a button-covering kit.

> ## TIPS
>
> Instead of free-motion machine embroidery, fill in the spaces with random stitches hand-embroidered with variegated floss.
>
> ✠ ✠ ✠
>
> Embellish the people: add fibers, beads, or other details.

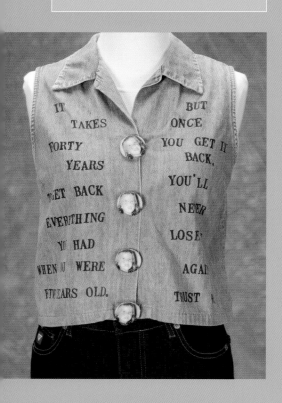

EMPRESS OF THE UNIVERSE

BY RICË FREEMAN-ZACHERY

Materials

- cotton chambray shirt
- iron-on transfers (you can take your photos to a copy shop to have this done or make them yourself with your computer, scanner, inkjet printer, and transfer paper)
- soft chalks
- fabric paint (featured, Neopaque)
- scrap of fabric
- fusible webbing
- covered buttons
- beads

Tools

- scissors
- pins
- button covering kit
- stamps
- foam brush
- cotton swabs
- iron and ironing board
- sewing machine or needle and thread
- embroidery needle and thread
- beading needle

Techniques

- ripping and tearing
- mending
- stamping with fabric paint
- image transfers
- heat setting
- painting fabric
- appliqué
- embroidery
- beading
- buttons

When I look at photos of myself as a child, I can remember how it felt to be in charge of the world. This journal shirt tells about how you know everything when you're five but somehow lose all that knowledge, self-confidence, and excitement as you grow up. The stamping says that after 40 years, you remember it, and that once you find all of that again, it's yours for the rest of your life. The last line on the front says, "Trust me." And when people read it and ask why they should trust me, I turn around and show them the back, where there's a picture taken on my fifth birthday, when I was, indeed, *Empress of the Universe*.

1   Alter the shirt if necessary. This was a hip-length shirt, cut off to a little below waist-length, and hemmed on the sewing machine.

2   Stamp the words on your shirt, using fabric paint, and set it aside to cure for 48 hours before heat setting. You may want to wait to stamp the back until you've completed the larger transfer and have prepared it as an appliqué so you can use it to determine the placement of the words stamped around it.

3   While you're waiting for the paint to dry, prepare your transfers—a larger one for the back and smaller ones for the buttons. I used the same photo for all the transfers here, but you can use a different one for each button, and you can add smaller transfers to the front of the shirt. Add color to parts of the transfers, as shown on the cheeks and dress in this project. (See Tips for Transfers, page 36.)

4   Iron the transfers on muslin, remove the sheen (See Image Transfers, page 35), and turn under the edges of the large transfer to prepare as an appliqué. Press the edges with the iron, being sure to cover the transfer itself with waxed paper.

5   Cover the buttons with the smaller transfers, following the pattern and instructions on the button covering kit.

6   After 48 hours, heat set the paint used to stamp the words.

7   Iron fusible webbing to the scrap of fabric and cut out a crown shape. Iron it over the top of the head of the transfer, being careful not to touch the transfer with the hot iron.

8   Appliqué the large transfer to the back of the shirt. You can use embroidery thread for a decorative edge or one of the other methods in Appliqués on page 40.

9   Embroider around the larger stamped letters.

10   Add beads as desired.

11   Sew on the buttons. (The buttons in the sample are far too large to be functional, so they were sewn in place over the buttonholes.)

template

COWGIRL SHRINE VEST, PAGE 108

SHRINE TEMPLATE

resources

UNITED STATES

Dharma Trading Company
Tel: 800.542.5227
www.dharmatrading.com
Email: info@dharmatrading.com

This is an excellent resource for everything you need to make artwear. In addition to a full line of Jacquard paints and dyes (my favorite), Dharma carries other brands of colorants, and almost everything else you can think of, including clothing blanks and fabric. The staff is helpful and friendly, and the catalog is a lot of fun, with instructions and commentary from real people who use the products and enjoy what they're doing. It's black-and-white but has color charts for the paints and dyes. The catalog is free.

Jacquard
Rupert, Gibbon and Spider, Inc.
P.O. Box 425
Healdsburg, CA 95448 USA
Tel: 800.442.0455
www.jacquardproducts.com

Wonderful paints, dyes, and powdered pigments for wearable art. Their line includes Lumiere, Neopaque, and Dye-Na-Flow. You can order directly from them or from Dharma, and often you can find their products at your local stamp store or craft store. Their catalog is beautiful—with full-color samples as well as charts of colors—and it's free. Call the toll-free number to order.

OTHER PAINTS AND INKS

Clearsnap
Tel: 800.448.4862

Dr. Ph. Martin's
Tel: 800.843.8293
www.docmartins.com
Email: docmartins@docmartins.com

Ranger Industries, Inc.
Tel: 800.244.2211
www.rangerink.com

Tsukineko
Tel: 800.769-6633
www.tsukineko.com

FABRIC STAMPS

Duncan
www.duncancrafts.com
Tel: 800.438.6226
Tel: 555.291.444

Check out their line of funky stamps.

Rubberstampede
www.rubberstampede.com

Foam stamps that are great on fabric—some nice design elements.

RUBBER STAMPS

There are a lot of sources for alphabet stamps, but here are three of my favorites:

Junque
P.O. Box 2378
Providence, RI 02906 USA
www.junque.net

Ma Vinci's Reliquary
P.O. Box 472702
Aurora, CO 80047-2702 USA
www.crafts.dm.net/mall/reliquary/
Email: MVReliquary@juno.com

Don't let the web address fool you—there are a LOT of alphabets here, well-presented and great fun to look at.

100 Proof Press
P.O. Box 299
Athens, OH 45701 USA
Tel: 740.594.2315
Fax: 800.511.2100
www.100proofpress.com

They offer about 25 unmounted alphabets, but these don't appear on the website. Catalogs are available for $4, refundable with an order.

SOURCES FOR STAMPS
USED IN PROJECTS

Hero Arts
Tel: 800.822.4376
Fax: 800.441.3632
www.heroarts.com

Hot Potatoes
2805 Columbine Place
Nashville, TN 37204 USA
Tel: 615.269.8002
Fax: 615.269.8004
www.hotpotatoes.com

Judikins
Tel: 310.515.1115
Fax: 310.323.6619
www.judikins.com

Posh Impressions
2260 Lambert Street, Suite 706
Lake Forest, CA 92630 USA
Tel: 800.421.POSH (7674)
Fax: 800.422.POSH (7674)
www.poshimpressions.com

Stampers Anonymous Stamps
The Creative Block
Tel: 440.250.9112
Tel: 888.326.0012 (outside Ohio)
Fax: 440.250.9117
www.stampersanonymous.com
Email: creativeblock@hotmail.com

Stampsmith Stamps
Tel: 631.547.5922
www.stampsmith.net
Email: estelle@stampsmith.com

Toybox Rubber Stamps
P.O. Box 1487
Healdsburg, CA 95448 USA
Tel: 707.431.1400
Fax: 707.431.2408
www.toyboxart.com

FABRICS

See Dharma Trading Company, above

Thai Silks!
www.thaisilks.com

Silk clothing blanks

SUPPLIES

Artfabrik
www.artfabrik.com

Check out their fabrics and hand-dyed threads.

Dick Blick
Tel: 800.447.8192 (ordering)
Tel: 800.723.2787 (customer service)
Tel: 800.933.2542 (product information)
www.dickblick.com

My source for Lumocolor pens. Also carries paints, inks, carving materials, etc.

Dover Publications
Tel: 516.742.6953
www.doverpublications.com

Free clip art catalog, sources for great copyright-free images.

Golden Paint
www.goldenpaint.com
Email: goldenart@goldenpaints.com
Source for matte medium, paints, etc.

Lucky Squirrel
P.O. Box 606
Belen, NM 87002 USA
Tel: 505.861.5606
www.luckysquirrel.com

Source for really great artist's grade shrink plastic. Check out their website for instructions on using shrink plastic, as well as for samples and inspiration.

Jerry's Sewing Machine Clinic
Odessa, TX USA
Tel: 432.580.4823

If you're ever in West Texas and looking for sewing machine help, this is the place to go. If not, check your area for a repair shop that sells used machines. I've bought two from Jerry and his wife—one for blanket stitching and one for free-motion embroidery, both at a fraction of the price I'd have paid for a fancy new model. They'll let you try out the machine before you buy and will provide information, support, and accessories. If you're just starting to sew, make friends with your local repair person—they can guide you through almost anything.

Nasco
Tel: 800.545.6566
www.enasco.com

Paints, inks, and carving materials

The Textile Workshop
www.thetextileworkshop.com

Fine hand-printed fabrics and hand-dyed rayon.

UK AND EUROPE

Creative Crafts
11 The Square
Winchester, Hampshire SO23 9ES UK
Tel: 01962 856266
www.creativecrafts.co.uk

Dylon International Ltd.
Worsley Bridge Road
Lower Sydenham
London SE26 5HD UK
Tel: 020 8663 4801
www.dylon.co.uk

(Click on the international link on the homepage to find distributors in your country.)

HobbyCraft
Head Office
Bournemouth UK
Tel: 1202 596 100

Stores throughout the UK

John Lewis
Flagship Store
Oxford Street
London W1A 1EX UK
Tel: 207 629 7711
www.johnlewis.co.uk

Stores throughout the UK

T N Lawrence & Son Ltd.
208 Portland Road
Hove BN3 5QT UK
Tel: 0845 644 3232
www.lawrence.co.uk
Email: artbox@lawrence.co.uk

AUSTRALIA AND NEW ZEALAND

Annaleey Crafts
P.O. Box 66
Yeelanna SA 5632
Tel: 08 8676 5026
Email: Stamps@Annaleeycrafts.com.au

Aussie Stamps & Crafts
4 Brougham Place
Golden Grove SA 5125
Tel: 08 82898871
Email: Mwo@lweb.net.au

Black Cat Creations
P.O. Box 489
Everton Park QLD 4053
Tel: 07 3354 4411

Bumble Bee Crafts
7 Toolara Street
The Gap QLD 4061
Tel: 07 3511 0068
Email: Buzz@Gil.com.au

Eckersley's Arts, Crafts, and Imagination
Tel: (300) 657 766 (catalog)
www.eckersleys.com.au

Stores located in New South Wales, Queensland, South Australia, and Victoria

Littlejohns Art & Graphic Supplies Ltd
170 Victoria Street
Wellington New Zealand
Tel: 04 385 2099
Fax: 04 385 2090

further reading

A-Z of Embroidery Stitches
Country Bumpkin Publications, 1997
ISBN 0646322025

Spiral-bound, this illustrated (with full-color step-by-step photographs) book is perfect for anyone learning embroidery. It includes everything from the split stitch and stem stitch to silk ribbon embroidery. Easy to follow, plus it lies flat so you can actually use it while you practice.

The Art Doll Chronicles:
A Collaborative Journey of Discovery
Stampington & Company, 2002
ISBN 0971729603

This book chronicles the collaboration of nine artists, including Keely Barham and Ricë Freeman-Zachery. Lavishly illustrated with detailed photographs of the dolls and their accompanying journals, it has lots of fabric work and is a visual and inspirational delight.

Beaded Embellishment: Techniques and Designs for Embroidering on Cloth
Amy C. Clarke and Robin Atkins
Interweave Press, 2002
ISBN 1931449128

Excellent book both for instruction and inspiration, with detailed illustrated instructions for embroidering with beads and lovely full-color photographs of completed projects.

Color on Paper and Fabric
Ruth Issett
Hand Book Press, 1999
ISBN 1893164020

This a good book for learning about color and dyeing fabric. It includes information about using metallic powders and acrylic mediums and has a very interesting section on glass plate printing on fabric.

Complex Cloth:
A Comprehensive Guide to Surface Design
Jane Dunnewold
Fiber Studio Press, 1996
ISBN 1564771490

The definitive guide to surface design, with detailed instructions for techniques ranging from bleach discharge to dyeing and from stenciling to adding foils.

Creating with Paint:
New Ways, New Materials
Sherrill Kahn
Martingale and Company, Inc., 2001
ISBN 1564773205

Wonderful techniques for painting on fabric, done in Sherrill's familiar, colorful style.

Creative Stamping with
Mixed Media Techniques
Sherrill Kahn
North Light Press, 2003
ISBN 1581803478

Focuses on how to use paint and rubber stamps to create backgrounds and patterns for use in wearable art.

Dyes and Paints:
A Hands-On Guide to Coloring Fabric
Elin Noble
Martingale and Company, Inc., 1998
ISBN 1564771032

Good guide for dying and painting fabrics. Technically very concise, with sidebars to provide tips and experiments. Lots of great photos of finished work for inspiration.

Exploring Textile Arts:
The Ultimate Guide to Manipulation, Coloring, and Embellishing Fabrics
The Editors of Creative Publishing International, Inc.
Creative Publishing International, Inc., 2002
ISBN 15889230485

Although it doesn't have an author, this book does have a lot of information, along with some really inspiring, well-photographed sample garments. I was especially intrigued by the section on pin-weaving—something new to try!

Fabric Painting: A Simple Approach
Ginny Eckley
Martingale and Company, Inc., 2000
ISBN 1564772950

The Fabric Stamping Handbook
Jean Ray Laury
C&T Publishing, 2002
ISBN 1571201300

All the information you need to get started stamping on your clothing. I recommend anything written by Laury—thorough, well-presented, and illustrated with terrific examples created by talented artists.

Fiberarts Design Books 1–6
Lark Books
by Fiberarts Magazine

Some of these are out of print and hard to find, but I've been successful in getting all six of them. They come out every couple of years and have sections on surface design, tapestry, quilts, and of course, wearable art. No instructions, just great ideas from the photographs (although it would be nice to have them larger, with more detail).

Fruits
Foreword and photographs by Shoici Aoki
Phaidon Press Limited, 2001
ISBN 0714840831

Full-page, full-color photographs of teenagers wearing Japanese street fashion. Great eye candy for anyone thinking about a new way to dress, and lots of fun to look at. Minimal text (just information about the kids wearing the clothing) that's hard to read—colored text on photographic background. But it doesn't matter—this is just a fun book, brought to my attention by doll artist Charla Khanna, who says it's a must for anyone interested in funky, alternative artwear.

Imagery on Fabric:
A Complete Surface Design Handbook
Jean Ray Laury
C&T Publishing, 1997 (2nd Edition)
ISBN 1571200347

If you can buy only one book—besides the one you're holding—this is the one to get. I love this book and have had it since the first edition came out in 1992. Laury provides instructions, tips, troubleshooting help, and samples of every method imaginable for getting images onto fabric. I can't say enough about this book—I own two copies.

Mickey Lawler's Skydyes:
A Visual Guide to Fabric Painting
Mickey Lawler, Rose Sheifer, Annie Nelson
C&T Publishing, 1999
ISBN 157120072X

Native Funk and Flash:
An Emerging Folk Art
Alexandra Jacopetti
Scrimshaw Press, 1974
ISBN 0912020377

This one's out of print, but if you can find a copy somewhere, get it. My favorite book ever for inspiration (no instructions) and just pure funkiness.

One Bead at a Time: Exploring Creativity with Bead Embroidery
Robin Atkins
Tiger Press, 2000
ISBN 097055382X

Another really great bead book, with photographs of completed pieces and text encouraging experimentation in freeform bead embroidery. This is the first book; Beaded Embellishment is the instructional book that came later.

Photo Transfer Handbook
Jean Ray Laury
C&T Publishing, 1999
ISBN 1571200649

More for the artist just beginning to use photographs on fabric, with a lot of examples using just photographs. If you can get only one of her books, opt for Imagery on Fabric, rather than this one. I buy them all—she's my transfer guru—but you don't have to have this one.

Stamp Artistry: Combining Stamps with Beadwork, Carving, Collage, Etching, Fabric, Metalwork, Painting, Polymer Clay, Repoussee, and More
Ricë Freeman-Zachery
Rockport Publishers, 2003
ISBN 1592530117

My first book has several artwear pieces, including another Journal Skirt, and instructions for creating them.

Tricia Gold on Color
Tricia Gold
Rizzoli International Publications, 1993
ISBN 0847818772

Well organized and really helpful for choosing colors. Beautiful photography.

The Ultimate T-Shirt Book
Deborah Morgenthal
Lark Books, 1998
ISBN 1579900178

This is a great book, with full-color photographs of T-shirts decorated using batik, tie-dye, painting, marbling, stamping, and screen printing. Unlike some of the tacky T-shirts you've seen, these are shirts you'd love to wear. Great for inspiration.

INSPIRATIONAL BOOKS

These are not technically about fabric art or artwear, but I've found them to be filled with inspiration.

Altered Books, Collaborative Journals, and Other Adventures in Bookmaking
Holly Harrison
Rockport Publishers, 2003
ISBN 1564969959

Something about art journals always inspires ideas for artwear. This book has great ideas and lovely photographs of journal pages.

The Book of Tiki
Sven A. Kirsten
Taschen Books, 2000
ISBN 382286417X

This is Allene Shackelford's favorite book on the art of the Tikis, and it provided the inspiration for her Tiki Art Jeans, page 96. "A really fun read for anyone interested in Polynesian Pop in 1950s America!"

True Colors: A Palette of Collaborative Art Journals
A Somerset Studio Publication
Stampington and Company, 2003
ISBN 0971729638

Gorgeous full-color photographs of collaborative art journals featuring art by a collection of talented artists. Keely Barham contributed to this book, and lots of her pages feature her terrific fabric art.

MAGAZINES

Belle Armoire
22992 Mill Creek, Suite B
Laguna Hills, CA 92653 USA
Tel: 949.380.9355
www.stampington.com

French for "pretty wardrobe," this magazine offers tips, techniques, artist profiles, and instructions for all kinds of artwear from clothes to shoes to jewelry.

Fiberarts Magazine
The Magazine of Textiles
Tel: 828.253.0467
Fax: 828.236.2869
www.fiberarts.com
Email: assteditor@fiberartsmagazine.com

Every once in a while I'll find something in here so stunning it sparks a new project.

Quilting Arts Magazine
www.quiltingarts.com

Always inspirational—this magazine features art quilts, rather than traditional quilts, and the techniques and ideas are eminently transferable to wearable art. They do include artwear, as well as art dolls. A great magazine.

Threads
Tel: 203.426.8171
Fax: 203.426.3434
www.taunton.com

Information, tips, ideas, and instructions for sewing. Can seem daunting to the beginner, but a good place to look for instructions if you're serious about sewing.

STAMP CREDITS

Various alphabets were used on the garments in this book, some handcarved and some commercially produced. The latter are from various sources and are unmarked. See the Resource section, page 120, for contact information on these companies.

Autumn Leaf Sandals (page 64)
Posh Impressions
foam stamp leaf from craft store

Stamped Silk Scarf (page 78)
Stampers Anonymous
Stampsmith

Summertime Dress (page 90)
Hot Potatoes

Tiki Art Jeans (page 96)
Toybox Rubber Stamps

Asian Flair Purse (page 100)
Hero Arts
Judikins

contributing artists

Keely Barham
Anaheim, California USA
www.itsmysite.com/FabricFrogDesigns
Email: FabFrogDesigns@aol.com

Keely is a mixed-media artist and workshop teacher. She is mainly interested in fabric art and beading, but also works with polymer clay and paper arts. She has had things published in Rubberstampmadness, Somerset Studio, *and* Belle Armoire *and has participated in collaborative projects including* The Art Doll Chronicles *and* True Colors. *Her teaching schedule and contact information can be found on her website.*

Jennifer Crutcher
Dallas, Texas USA
www.yayadesigns.com
Email: jenifah@comcast.net

Jennifer has been sewing since she was seven years old. She makes and sells children's clothes and teaches classes at Stamp Asylum in Plano, Texas.

Lenna Andrews Foster
Tel: 860.413.9050
www.lennastamp.com
www.picturetrail.com/lennastamp (photo gallery)
Email: lenna1@cox.net

Lenna is a published mixed-media artist and instructor. She has been creating things since she was a child and just never stopped! You can find her work in Rubberstampmadness, Expression Magazine, Vamp Stamp News, The Rubber Stamper, ARTitude Zine, Belle Armoire, Somerset Studio, The Stamper's Sampler, *as well as in* The Stamp Artist's Project Book *(2001), and* Altered Books 101 *(2002). You can view her current teaching schedule and see her artwork on her website or Picture Trail Gallery.*

Leslie Gelber
Auburn, California USA
Email: les@gelber.com

Leslie Gelber is a studio artist living in Auburn, California. Her passion is art garb.

Laurie Mika
Encinitas, California USA
www.mikaarts.com

Laurie is a very "mixed up" media artist. Her work incorporates her passion for travel and her ongoing quest to find fragments, shards, and discarded items to embellish the surfaces of pieces she calls "Icons." Her work can best be described as mixed-media mosaics that also contain her unique handmade tiles. Laurie has been published and sells her work through galleries and juried shows.

Lesley Riley
Bethesda, Maryland USA
www.LaLasLand.com
Email: LRileyART@aol.com

Lesley Riley's art is inspired by the fabric of our lives. Fabric is an integral part of every creation, whether it is used to tell a story or employed simply to celebrate its inherent beauty. The endless supply of fabric provides Lesley with a never-ending source of inspiration. Her work has appeared in numerous books, magazines, and shows and is collected by art lovers all over the world. She teaches workshops and can be contacted by email for information on scheduling.

Anne Sagor

Garland, Texas USA

Email: sooie@juno.com

Formerly an English teacher, Anne Sagor now happily teaches rubber-stamping related classes at Stamp Asylum in Plano, Texas. Her work has been featured in Rubberstampmadness *and has appeared in* Stamper's Sampler *and* Somerset Studio, *as well as the book* Stamp Artistry. *She creates samples for several major rubber stamp companies.*

Allene Shackelford

Healdsburg, California USA

Tel: 707.431.1400

www.toyboxart.com

Allene Shackelford is the owner/artist of Toybox Rubber Stamps. Her techniques and unique artwork have been featured in many publications, books, and videos. Allene's background also includes teaching, quilting, stamping, and jewelry making.

Roz Stendahl

Minneapolis, Minnesota USA

www.rozworks.com

Email: roz@rozworks.com

Roz Stendahl is a graphic designer, illustrator, and writer. She has been keeping visual and written journals since childhood. She teaches book arts, beading, journaling, and art classes. Please view her website for samples of her journals and mixed-media art, as well as her class listings.

Lynn Whipple

Winter Park, Florida USA

www.whippleart.com

Email: jxlwhipple@aol.com

Lynn Whipple is a nationally known mixed-media artist whose found-object-inspired works include collage, waxed garments, drawing, painting, altered images, assemblages, and installations. Lynn's work has been seen in such publications as ME Home Companion, New American Paintings, Lark Books, *and* Communication Arts. *Lynn and artist husband John enjoy traveling and showing their work nationally in juried shows and art galleries. To find a listing of upcoming shows, art projects, and workshops, please visit www.whippleart.com.*

Linda Woods

Valencia, California USA

www.colormetrue.com

www.sistersonsojourn.com

Linda Woods is a mixed-media artist whose travel-inspired artworks have appeared in numerous publications. As Linda sojourns to teach workshops in the United States and abroad, she shares her tips for travel, art, and artful journaling through her websites.

about the author

Ricë Freeman-Zachery has been designing and altering her clothes for as long as she can remember. She creates journal skirts and other wearable art and teaches artwear at workshops around the country. Her art has appeared in various books and magazines.

As a freelance writer, she has written for *Art Doll Quarterly, Belle Armoire, Cat Fancy, Legacy, Personal Journaling, Rubberstampmadness,* and *Somerset Studio.* Her first book, *Stamp Artistry,* was published in 2003.

She works out of her home studio in Midland, Texas, where she lives with her husband, Earl, and an impressive herd of cats.

And, yes, she really does wear these clothes in public.

She'd love to see photos of your artwear! Contact her at rice.freeman-zachery@att.net.

Photograph by Earl Zachery

acknowledgments

Thank you to all the artists who contributed artwear to these pages. Their generosity in providing not only their garments but also instructions for making those garments is amazing in a world filled with competition. Their spirit of sharing is an inspiration to artists everywhere, and their creativity is a continuous joy.

I'd also like to thank:
My editor, Mary Ann Hall, for believing there is enough interest in artwear to warrant a book like this one. Her hard work in convincing everyone else is the reason it exists.

My mother, Betty Freeman, for passing on her love of fabric and sewing and creating garments that look nothing like the clothes worn by anyone else. She never pushed me to learn to sew, but the hours I spent sitting at her feet on the floor of her sewing room, playing with scraps of fabric, must have taught me something, perhaps by osmosis. She's still the person I call when my sewing machine acts up or I can't remember how to make a buttonhole.

Lynne Perrella, whose generosity and spirit of inclusion have presented me with opportunities I would never have had otherwise. She's that rare combination of an astounding artistic talent and solid logical sense.

My husband, Earl, who cheerfully puts up with unimaginable household messes and isn't bothered in the least that other people think his wife dresses just the tiniest bit oddly. When he's not busy teaching or coaching basketball, he's happy to pin hems, untangle thread, and wander the miles of exhibits at the International Quilt Show. What a guy!